CRIME:

INVESTIGATION & EVIDENCE

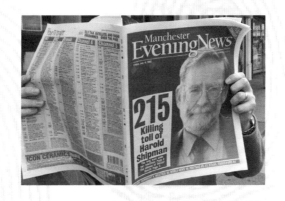

This is a **FLAME TREE** book
First published 2010

Publisher and Creative Director: Nick Wells
Senior Project Editor: Catherine Taylor
Editorial: Sonya Newland
Art Director: Mike Spender
Layout Design: Dave Jones
Digital Design and Production: Chris Herbert
Proofreader: Dawn Laker
Indexer: Helen Snaith

Special thanks to Sara Robson

11 13 14 12 10
1 3 5 7 9 10 8 6 4 2

This edition first published 2010 by
FLAME TREE PUBLISHING
Crabtree Hall, Crabtree Lane
Fulham, London SW6 6TY
United Kingdom

www.flametreepublishing.com

Flame Tree is part of the Foundry Creative Media Co. Ltd

ISBN 978-1-84786-965-4

A CIP record for this book is available from the British Library upon request.

Printed in China

Picture Credits
Getty Images: 157, 179, 226; Sean Gallup: 44; John Chapple: 156; Bernard Kane: 158;
Craig Strong: 159; Chris Livingston: 120. **Mary Evans Picture Library**: 27, 28, 32, 150, 146, 123,
124, 128, 129. **Science Photo Library**: Volker Steger, Peter Arnold Inc.: 238; Volker Steger: 243
All other pictures courtesy of Topham Picturepoint, and collections from AP, The British
Library/HIP, Fotomas, Image Works, Novosti, PA, Photonews, PressNet, Star Images, UPP, UPPA Ltd.

CRIME:

INVESTIGATION & EVIDENCE

JON & DIANE SUTHERLAND

Introduction:
BARRY PRITCHARD

FLAME TREE
PUBLISHING

Contents

Kings, presidents, prime ministers and all manner of other public figures have been targets for assassins for centuries. With the development of guns and bombs, however, incidents of these murders – or attempted murders – have increased. This chapter looks at some of the best-known assassinations and attempts, from JFK to John Lennon.

Multiple Murders...............................36

Since the days of Bonnie and Clyde, people have been fascinated and horrified by the actions of mass murderers. The indiscriminate killing of people on the streets and in schools has left a lasting impact on the communities affected. From deliberate mass murder to frenzied spree killing, this section covers some of the most notorious incidents of multiple murder in history.

Serial Killers...............................54

Since the days of Jack the Ripper, serial killers have caused fear around the globe. Sometimes targeted, sometimes seemingly indiscriminate, the murders appear to be calculated and cold. This chapter looks at some of the highest profile cases of serial killing and investigates the techniques used to catch and try the murderers.

More than 90 per cent of murders are carried out by men, and this chapter looks at some of the worst of them. From wife-killers to opportunistic murderers, seizing women or children at random, these are the cases and killers that made headline news.

From the nineteenth-century case of Clara Ford to the trial and execution of Ruth Ellis – the last woman hanged in Britain – this chapter investigates some of the most notorious female killers of all time, and proves that, in some cases at least, the female of the species is indeed deadlier than the male.

Crime rates are rising among the young. Today, more than ever before, young people – some not even in their teens – are acquiring guns and other weapons and using them against their parents and their peers. From the infamous case of Lizzie Borden to the Columbine school massacre, this chapter looks at the world's worst examples of child murderers.

Criminal gangs have operated across the world for many years, but some places have been particular hotbeds of organized crime, such as Chicago and New York. These murderous 'families' strike fear into the hearts of those who cross them, and their leaders have become some of the most notorious criminals in history.

Intriguing Cases

This chapter covers the cases that have baffled and intrigued investigators and the public alike, whether because of the sinister rituals involved or the questions hanging over the guilt – or innocence – of the accused.

Unsolved Murders

With modern investigative techniques, success rates in catching criminals are higher than ever before. But justice is not always served, and some killers are never caught. From Jack the Ripper to the conspiracy theories that surround the death of Marilyn Monroe, this section covers the cases that still haunt us.

Investigative Techniques and Punishment 232

Today, forensic science is key to establishing the guilt – or innocence – of a suspect. Technology is so advanced that scientists can discover evidence from the smallest amount of trace evidence in particles of dust or human skin. This chapter looks at the techniques used to convict killers, as well as the forms of punishment meted out.

Introduction

Crime: Investigation & Evidence is a collection of tales about all aspects of the
criminal world. It brings together cases, both notorious and little known, to offer
an enthralling compendium of true crime.

Criminal Curiosity

There has always been a universal fascination with stories of crimes and criminals. Who
knows the cause? Maybe it is to do with law-abiding citizens' curiosity as to how others have
flouted the conventions of society in a way they would never do, or because they provide an
insight into human psychology and behaviour. Perhaps it is an escape from everyday life: as
a species, we are curious, and who could not fail to feel the slightest twinge of intrigue at the
details of the latest murder trial covering the front pages of our morning newspaper?

The Sensationalization of Crime

Prior to stories of true crime being printed in books and newspapers, accounts of sensational
crimes of the day were spread through other media. Verses and ballads from the sixteenth to
nineteenth centuries gave gory details of crimes with moralistic overtones and, occasionally,
criminals would write 'true confessions' themselves. The advent of the daily newspaper
meant that information about criminal activity could be spread easily to a wide audience, a
practice which continues unabated today. When the judicial process shifted to trial by
evidence rather than confession, there was a whole new series of events to include in the
newspaper accounts: the search for evidence, interviewing of witnesses, locating the suspect
and the trial itself, at which evidence is displayed and witnesses are presented. When police
forces were first formed, the detectives became the main investigators in criminal cases.
From then on, many accounts, both fictional and real, were based upon their work.

Today, people are more interested than ever in the workings of the criminal mind:
countless films and books are based on real crimes, and many criminals, such as Bonnie and

Detectives discover another victim of the Yorkshire Ripper.

Clyde, Myra Hindley, and Fred and Rosemary West are virtually household names. Turn on the television, and you will see 'real life' criminal investigation programmes, drama series based on actual events, and re-enactments of crimes as an attempt to solve cases, both old and new. No day goes by without some kind of criminal activity being reported on our news bulletins. We live in a world where people are highly aware of the types of crime that go on around them, and are fascinated and fearful in turn.

The aftermath of the St Valentine's Day Massacre in 1929.

Famous Cases

True Crime embraces the scope of the criminal world. It is divided into sections that deal with particular aspects of crime, and looks at the most notorious or celebrated cases within each category over time. In organizing the book in this way, the authors succeed in showing how crime has evolved over the last three or four hundred years, and, in many cases, how frighteningly similar crimes committed today are to those committed three or more hundred years ago. Recent cases included are all too painful and familiar: the tragic case of the death of toddler James Bulger; the unbelievable extent of the murders committed by Dr Harold Shipman; the did-he-didn't-he intrigue of the O.J. Simpson case, and the seemingly random shootings of the Washington sniper. Looking to the past, it contains details of some notorious cases, including the cannibalistic Sawney Bean family and the elusive Jack the Ripper. Organized crime plays an increasingly large role in today's society, and the book includes a section on the organized crimes committed by gangsters over the past hundred years or so. Mass murderers, serial killers and spree killers from the past three centuries all have a place in the book, as do crimes committed by women and children and cases that remain unsolved.

The methods used to catch criminals have changed as scientific techniques have advanced. Where once a case was unsolvable, the perpetrator can now be caught using incriminating evidence such as a speck of saliva or a hair, thanks to forensic science and DNA testing. Punishment, too, has changed over time. *True Crime* looks at different investigative techniques, and at the types of capital punishment that have been meted out, past and present.

The Tragedy Behind the Truth

What one must not forget is that behind each of the stories in this book there lies a human tragedy – the death of the victim, the grief of those left behind, or even a miscarriage of justice for the accused. *True Crime* does not seek to glorify crime in any way; instead, by gathering together stories of real events from around the world, it presents a sickening and, at the same time, engrossing account of what drives people to commit crimes.

Barry Pritchard
Former Superintendent Operations, Salisbury

1

assassinations

Presidential
Assassinations

Holding the most high-profile and powerful position in the world means US presidents have been the frequent targets of assassins. The first attempt was on Andrew Jackson in 1835; this failed, but future presidents were not so lucky and four have lost their lives to an assassin's bullet.

Wilkes Booth, John (1865)

John Wilkes Booth, from Baltimore in Maryland, was a Confederate and operated as a spy and smuggler during the early years of the American Civil War, using his occupation as a touring actor for cover. In 1864, he began plotting the kidnap of Abraham Lincoln – the leader of the northern US states during the war – hoping to seize and exchange him for Confederate prisoners and munitions. The plan had to be abandoned in March 1865, however, when Lincoln changed his itinerary. Booth began again, though, only this time, he and his fellow conspirators planned to assassinate Lincoln, his vice-president Johnson and the secretary of state, Seward, on the night of 14 April 1865.

The Crime

Lincoln was attending a performance at the Ford Theatre in Washington, occupying the State Box with his wife and two close friends. Booth shot Lincoln in the head and then leapt down on to the stage, breaking a bone in his leg. Nonetheless, he effected his escape. Elsewhere, Seward was badly wounded but the attack on Johnson failed to materialize.

And Punishment

On 26 April, the conspirators were cornered at a firm in Port Royal, Virginia and, in the

A drawing of Abraham Lincoln's assassination at Ford Theatre

confrontation, Booth was mortally wounded. On 29 June, his co-plotters were found guilty and sentenced to hang on 7 July. Among them was Mary Surratt, the first African-American woman to be executed.

See Lee Harvey Oswald p. 19

Guiteau, Charles (1881)

Charles Guiteau was something of a religious crank, but this did not prevent his entry into US politics. He was part of the unsuccessful campaign for the Democrat presidential candidate, Horace Greely, in 1872. In 1880, he supported Ulysses S. Grant, who also lost. Guiteau then switched his allegiance to the successful James Garfield and firmly believed that the new president should reward him with a political post.

Frustration Leads to Murder

For some months after Garfield's election, Guiteau pestered staff at the White House, certain that Garfield would reward his loyalty. At first, he was seen as something of a joke, but he soon gained a reputation as a pest. When no post was forthcoming, Guiteau became frustrated and determined to eliminate the man who was hindering his political career. He shot Garfield on 2 July 1881. Garfield lingered between life and death for several months, and finally died on 19 December. Still basking in the limelight, Guiteau was executed in June 1882.

Czolgosz, Leon Franz (1901)

Polish-American Leon Czolgosz was fascinated by the newspaper accounts of Gaetano Bresci's assassination of King Humbert I in July 1900. Czolgosz was determined to gain for himself the same degree of fame. He bought himself a pistol and headed off to the Pan-American Exposition in Buffalo, with the intention of killing the president, William McKinley.

Two Deaths

On 6 September 1901, Czolgosz joined a queue of people waiting to shake hands with McKinley. When he reached the head of the queue, he shot McKinley in the abdomen and chest. Arrested immediately, Czolgosz refused to speak and remained silent throughout his trial. He was sentenced to death by electrocution; acid was then poured into his coffin to destroy his body. Czolgosz was the first assassin to be executed by electrocution.

Leon Czolgosz shoots US President McKinley at the Pan–American Exposition in Buffalo.

Schrank, John (1912)

US presidential candidate Theodore Roosevelt's short-sightedness and his habit of delivering long-winded speeches undoubtedly saved his life in 1912. John Schrank, a psychotic New York barkeeper, attempted to kill Roosevelt during a stop in Milwaukee as part of his presidential election campaign. Schrank had aimed for Roosevelt's head, but a bystander spoiled his aim at the last second. Roosevelt did not even realize he had been shot until someone noticed a hole in his overcoat. The bullet had passed through a double-folded 50-page speech script and his spectacle case before entering his body, lodging in his chest wall. The assassination attempt ruined Roosevelt's chances of election and he lost to William Taft. Schrank was committed to a mental institution in Wisconsin, where he died in 1943 without ever having received a visitor.

See Samuel S. Byck p. 21

Zangara, Giuseppe (1933)

Italian-born Giuseppe Zangara blamed American president Franklin D. Roosevelt for privations suffered during the Depression. On 15 February 1933, while the president was visiting Bayfront Park in Chicago, Zangara pushed his way into the crowd, armed with a revolver. Being short, he had to stand on a chair. Zangara missed Roosevelt, but hit the Chicago mayor and four onlookers. Although Zangara was initially sentenced to 84 years imprisonment, this was subsequently changed to the death sentence after the mayor succumbed to his injuries and died. Zangara was executed on 20 March 1933.

Oswald, Lee Harvey (1963)

Lee Harvey Oswald was the alleged assassin of President John F. Kennedy. He was a former US Marine and had lived in the Soviet Union between 1959 and 1962, where he had married a Russian national. He returned to the US and became involved in pro-Castro Cuban politics. Officially at least, he shot Kennedy from the sixth floor of the Texas Schoolbook Depository, where he was employed, in Dallas at around 12.30 p.m. on 22 November 1963.

Oswald's Assassination

Shortly afterwards, he was arrested and, from the outset, he denied that he had shot anyone. Two days later, whilst being transferred to another prison, Oswald was assassinated by Jack Ruby. This act only sought to muddy the waters even further, as it is widely believed by many that Oswald did not, in fact, fire the fatal shots and that Ruby had killed Oswald to prevent the truth ever being disclosed.

The Warren Commission

The Warren Commission was set up in November 1963 to investigate the assassination, but, to this date, their findings have remained secret, simply fuelling the belief that Kennedy was assassinated as the result of some elaborate conspiracy. Officially, Oswald remains the prime candidate, but many believe that one day the truth will be revealed.

Ruby, Jack (1963)

Two days after Oswald had been arrested for assassinating President Kennedy, this Dallas nightclub owner assassinated the assassin. Ruby was of Polish extraction and had been involved in organised crime from a fairly young age. He habitually carried a gun and claimed that his assassination of Oswald was a spur-of-the-moment decision.

The Kennedy Conspiracy

The actual assassination was broadcast live on American television. Ruby initially claimed that he had killed Oswald to save Jacqueline Kennedy the trauma of testifying at the trial, but many believe that Ruby was part of a larger mafia conspiracy and his task was to silence Oswald.

On 14 March 1964, Ruby was found guilty of Oswald's murder, but the conviction was overturned and, before he could be retried, he died of cancer in prison on 3 January 1967.

Nightclub owner Jack Ruby, seconds before shooting Lee Harvey Oswald in the stomach.

Byck, Samuel S. (1974)

Samuel S.Byck was a failed businessman who believed that the US political system was corrupt. He had begun threatening President Nixon by mail in 1972 but, on 22 February 1974, he launched his plan 'Operation Pandora's Box' with the intention of hijacking an airliner and crashing it into the White House. He shot his way on to a jet at the Baltimore-Washington airport. The plane was unable to lift off, so he shot the pilot and co-pilot; faced with capture, he committed suicide.

Fromme, Lynette (1975)

Lynette Fromme was a disciple of Charles Manson. When Manson was sentenced to life imprisonment, she feared he would be forgotten, so she determined to assassinate President Gerald Ford to remind people that Manson's 'family' still lived. On 5 September 1975, she attempted Ford's murder in Sacramento, but had not correctly loaded her gun and was wrestled to the ground. She was sentenced to life but escaped from a prison in San Diego. Since her recapture, she has been held in maximum-security prisons in West Virginia, Lexington and Florida.

See Charles Manson p. 86

Hinckley, John Warnock Jr (1981)

Oklahoma-born John Hinckley was obsessed with the actress Jodie Foster, and equally fascinated with assassination. He was fined for possession of handguns whilst stalking President Carter in 1980, then determined to shoot the new president, Ronald Reagan, detailing the 'historic deed' in a letter to Foster. Outside Washington's Hilton, Hinckley fired six shots; one hit Reagan in the chest and three other people were wounded. Hinckley, not guilty due to insanity, was sent to St Elizabeth's Institution in Washington.

President Reagan is helped into the Presidential Limousine after being shot in 1981.

Political Assassinations

Apart from presidents, many other political figures have been targets for assassination all over the globe. The assassins' motives range from ideology to insanity, but, whatever the driving force, attempts on the lives of political figures send shockwaves around the world.

McNaghten, Daniel (1843)

In 1843, Daniel McNaghten, a Scottish woodworker, attempted to kill the British prime minister, Robert Peel, but instead assassinated Peel's secretary, Edward Drummond. McNaghten believed that the government was plotting against him. In a landmark case, the defendant was acquitted on the grounds that he was insane, the opinion of nine experts. McNaghten was committed to the Bethlehem Hospital (Bedlam) and later to Broadmoor.

Diminished Responsibility

This case pioneered the idea that, while all defendants are considered sane at the outset of their trials, if this is later proved otherwise, they cannot be deemed responsible for their actions. The concept was later adopted by most Commonwealth countries and some states in America. The crucial point in such cases was the defendants' incapacity to understand the severity of their actions – in other words, a diminished responsibility for what they had done.

The Killing of Juan Prim (1870)

An unknown assassin shot Juan Prim, the Spanish prime minister, in December 1870, as he was leaving the Madrid government chamber. Prim was a Liberal and a monarchist, and was known to have innumerable opponents in the more reactionary right-wing side of Spanish politics. There is little doubt that clandestine reactionary forces were behind the assassination and that this assisted in ensuring that the killer was never identified.

Ravochol (1892)

In 1892, Ravochol, or François-Cladius Koeningstein, took action against the French government after the violent suppression by the police of a labour rally in Clichy. He planted bombs at the homes of the presiding judge and prosecutor in the Clichy case, then bombed the Lobau Barracks in Paris; there were no deaths from the bombings. Identified at a Paris restaurant by a waiter and sentenced to life, Ravochol was later executed for two earlier killings. The restaurant was subsequently bombed by other anarchists.

See Robert François Damiens p. 27

Princip, Gavrilo (1914)

Gavrilo Princip was a Bosnian Serb who assassinated Franz Ferdinand, Archduke of Austria and the heir to the Austro-Hungarian throne. The attack took place on 28 June 1914 and was undoubtedly one of the key events that led to the outbreak of World War the First.

Second Shot

Earlier in the day, there had been a Serbian bomb attack on the archduke, which had killed the driver and wounded the passengers in the car behind him. The archduke was heading for the hospital to

Gavrilo Princip, assassin of Archduke Franz Ferdinand in Sarajevo.

visit the victims when Princip seized his chance and shot Franz Ferdinand's wife Sophie in the head, and the archduke in the chest. Franz Ferdinand bled to death before the wound could be tended.

Outbreak of War

The Austrians demanded to be allowed to investigate the conspiracy in Serbia and, just one month later, the First World War began. Princip was a member of the pro-Serbian Young Bosnia Group, supplied by a secret organization known as the Black Hand, which had links with the Serbian government and military. Princip was given 20 years imprisonment for the murder of Franz Ferdinand and his wife on that fateful day in Sarajevo. Princip died of tuberculosis in prison on 28 April 1918.

See The Killing of Juan Prim p. 22

Von Stauffenberg, Claus (1944)

By the summer of 1944, the fortunes of Nazi Germany had turned irrevocably for the worse. For some time, there had been a smouldering resentment against Adolf Hitler and his leadership. It was therefore decided amongst certain circles of the German officer class to rid the country of its Führer.

Stauffenberg's Failure

Claus von Stauffenberg placed a bomb in a briefcase inside Hitler's command bunker in Rastenburg, Prussia; the weapon had been provided by German intelligence. The bomb failed to kill Hitler and the plot to seize power failed. Von Stauffenberg was shot

Claus von Stauffenberg, who attempted to assassinate Adolf Hitler in 1944.

and many of the conspirators were slowly put to death, their agonies filmed for Hitler's later delight. It has been estimated that some 20,000 people were killed or sent to concentration camps as a result of Hitler's purges after the attempt.

See Gavrilo Princip p. 23

Ray, James Earl (1968)

James Earl Ray assassinated the civil rights leader Martin Luther King Jr on 4 April 1968 at the Lorraine Motel in Memphis, Tennessee. Witnesses had placed Ray at the scene of the assassination, and suspicions about his guilt were compounded by the fact that he fled the country immediately after the event.

Apprehension and Evidence

He was apprehended at Heathrow Airport in London on 8 June. His fingerprints were found on the rifle and on a pair of binoculars that had been found at the scene of the crime, and he admitted to buying a similar rifle. He claimed that he had given the weapon to a man called Raoul; this man has never been traced. It was always believed that Ray had not acted alone.

Trial and Death

In court the following year, he pleaded guilty to the assassination, but just three days after he had been convicted of the killing and sentenced to 99 years, he withdrew his confession. Martin Luther King's son Dexter continually supported James Ray's demand for a retrial. He believed that his father and Ray were victims of a broader conspiracy. Ray died

James Earl Ray, Martin Luther King's killer, is escorted to a cell in Memphis, Tennessee.

from a kidney disease in 1998, as a result of receiving a blood transfusion following a stabbing incident in prison. To date, further investigations have proved inconclusive.

See Lee Harvey Oswald p. 19

Carlos the Jackal (1972-94)

Venezuelan-born Ilich Ramirez Sanchez, known as Carlos the Jackal, had a three-decade career of bombings, kidnappings, hijackings and assassinations. On 14 August 1994, living under an alias in Khartoum, Sudan, the Jackal was finally captured and transferred under heavy guard to Paris to face a catalogue of charges, including a car bombing in the centre of Paris in 1982. He was also charged with a grenade attack on an Israeli bank, being the mastermind behind the Munich Olympics atrocity in 1972, the seizing of hostages at the

Carlos the Jackal (Ilich Ramirez Sanchez) and various arms belonging to him.

OPEC meeting in Vienna in 1975 and numerous other crimes. He was to spend three years in solitary confinement before being sentenced to life for the murder of two French security agents and a Lebanese revolutionary in 1975.

See Secret Army Organization p. 34

The Killing of Benazir Bhutto (2007)

Former prime minister of Pakistan Benazir Bhutto returned to her native country in October 2007, after a period of exile following charges of corruption ousted her. On 27 December that year, she attended a campaign rally. As she left the rally in her bulletproof car, she stood up to wave at crowds through the sunroof, at which point she was shot at by a gunman. Bombs planted nearby exploded simultaneously, killing members of the public. It was claimed that she was not in fact killed by the hail of bullets, but by fracturing her skull while attempting to get back inside the car. Al-Qaeda took responsibility for the assassination.

See Lee Harvey Oswald p. 19

Royal Assassinations

Regicide (the deliberate murder of a monarch) has been carried out for centuries. Sometimes, it was carried out after a legal trial – such as in the case of the unfortunate Charles I – but more often, kings have been the unsuspecting targets for assassins.

Damiens, Robert François (1757)

In 1757, a half-witted crank named Robert Damiens made an attempt on the life of Louis XV of France. The French had already lost two kings to assassins: Henry III, who was stabbed to death in 1589, and Henry IV in 1610. These had been murders motivated by religion, but Damiens was simply crazed. He attacked the king with a blunt knife, failed to take the monarch's life, and was eventually torn to pieces by four horses – a fate reserved for those guilty of treason.

The execution, by quartering, of Robert François Damiens in 1757.

See Drawing and Quartering p. 247

Zhelyabov (1881)

Zhelyabov had attempted to assassinate Tsar Alexander II of Russia in February 1880, and even though this failed, he continued to plan the downfall of the monarch. Zhelyabov was captured at the end of February 1881, but, over the ensuing days, his anarchist followers struck again, using a bomb. The blast shattered the Tsar's legs and he died several days later. The anarchists had taken no chances, this time, planting assassins along all the rail routes out of St Petersburg.

Yurovsky, Yakob (1917)

Yakob Yurovsky's father was a criminal who had been deported to Siberia, and Yurovsky himself had joined the Bolsheviks in 1905. By 1918, he had become a leading member of the Bolshevik party and, in early July, he had been assigned the task of guarding the Russian royal family, who were being held prisoner.

Murder in the Basement

In July 1917, in the company of 10 militia, Yurovsky read the death sentence to Tsar Nicholas II in the basement of a house on the outskirts of Ekaterinburg. He shot the tsar and then his wife, Alexandra. The other members of the firing squad dispatched the rest of the family – the tsarevich Alexei and his four sisters – and their servants. The bodies were first left in an abandoned mine, but they were later reburied along a road when the truck carrying their corpses got stuck in mud.

The body of fatally wounded Tsar Alexander II is hurried back to the palace.

Last of the Russian Monarchy

This massacre was the culmination of a bitter struggle between the Bolsheviks and the White Army, still loyal to the Romanov royal family, and the events of the night of 17 July 1918 saw the end of the Russian monarchy. Yurovsky, a hero of the revolution, finally died after a long illness in1938.

Famous Assassinations

Political and royal leaders are not the only people in the spotlight. Celebrity attracts fans and fans can become obsessive. Famous faces of all kinds can draw the unwanted attention of those who disagree with their views or just simply want to use an attack on them to make a point.

Solanas, Valerie (1968)

Valerie Solanas was a militant feminist during the 1960s. In 1967, she had written a play entitled *The Scum Manifesto*, which rounded on men and expressed her opinion of their desire for power and money.

Assassination Attempt

Solanas had asked the Pop artist Andy Warhol to produce her play in 1967, but he had never responded to this request. She demanded the script's return from him; Warhol told her he had lost it and she began demanding money instead. On 3 June 1968, she entered his studio in New York and shot him three times, for which she received three years for attempted murder. Solanas became a drug addict and a prostitute after serving her prison sentence and died at the age of 52 in San Francisco.

Chapman, Mark David (1980)

Mark Chapman shot ex-Beatle John Lennon outside Lennon and Yoko Ono's New York apartment building, the Dakota, on 8 December 1980. Earlier that day, he had approached the couple and asked Lennon to sign a copy of his new album, *Double Fantasy*. At that point, his conscience got the better of him, but not enough to prevent him waiting until the pair returned, at which point Chapman sent four bullets into Lennon's back. Some people still believe that Chapman was not just a disturbed stalker, as it was thought at the time, but that he may have been part of a broader conspiracy to murder the pro-peace musician.

Chapman's Paranoia

Chapman believed that the lyrics in Lennon's songs were directed at him and, as a paranoid schizophrenic, he apparently could not ignore these signals. He was also reportedly disillusioned by the 'phoniness' of the super-rich star who preached peace and love over material wealth. As a born-again Christian, he is said to have been particularly angered by Lennon's 1966 comment that the Beatles had become 'more popular than Jesus'. Chapman admired the Beatles and so probably felt especially let down.

Conspiracy Theories

Lennon's son, Sean, believed that shadowy government officials had ordered the execution of his father. As a vocal civil rights and anti-Vietnam war activist Lennon had indeed been subject to FBI surveillance and an attempt in 1973 to deport him. It takes a little more suspension of disbelief, however, to believe – as one theory suggests – that Chapman was 'remotely controlled' to kill Lennon, by the use of a 'trigger', such as a copy of the novel, *The Catcher in the Rye*, that Chapman was obsessed with and pointed to as an explanation of his crime. Chapman was sentenced to 20 years imprisonment in 1980. He had his first parole request rejected in 2000 on the grounds that his killing of John Lennon was calculated and unprovoked. His most recent parole request in 2008 was denied 'due to concern for public safety and welfare'.

Agca, Mehmet Ali (1981)

Agca attempted to assassinate Pope John Paul II on 13 May 1981, but only succeeded in wounding him. Agca claimed to be a member of the Popular Front for the Liberation of Palestine, but they denied his membership of their group. He then claimed to be backed by the Bulgarians, who had been forced by the KGB to launch an assassination attempt in response to the Pope's support for the Polish Solidarity Movement. No clear link or motive was ever established. Agca was sentenced to life, but, in June 2000, he was pardoned by the Italian president, Carlo Azeglio Ciampi, and deported to Turkey, where he spent more time in prison for the murder of a newspaper editor. He was released in January 2010.

Police Murders

Because they are public figures, the murder of police officers is considered assassination. Often, these people are not the main targets of assassins, but find themselves caught in dangerous situations facing desperate criminals. Sometimes, however, police officers are deliberately chosen to die because of their position.

The Murder of PC Grantham (1830)

The first English policeman to lose his life while in uniform was PC Grantham, on 29 June 1830. Grantham was on duty in north London that evening, when he intervened in a fight between two Irishmen. The two men, and a woman who was with them, stabbed Grantham until he fell to the ground and then violently kicked him several times. He died soon afterwards and the perpetrators were never brought to justice.

See The Murder of PC Blakelock p. 33

The Tottenham Outrage (1909)

In 1909, two Eastern European anarchists attempted to snatch the payroll from a factory in Tottenham, London. The wage clerk refused to co-operate and shots were fired. Soon, the gunmen were being chased through the streets by unarmed policemen.

Anarchists on the Streets

The gunmen fired back at the policemen, missing their targets but killing a young boy. When they reached Chingford Road, the gunmen jumped on a passing tram. During the ride, they shot and wounded one of the passengers and, as they leapt off the tram, they also injured a milkman. They then made off on a horse-drawn grocer's van, chased by policemen on bicycles and armed with cutlasses.

The Outcome of the Outrage

Both men were later cornered, but committed suicide after the two-hour chase, which had covered six miles. The incident had cost the lives of one policeman and a child, as well as seven police and 14 civilians wounded.

See The Houndsditch Killings and the Sidney Street Siege p. 39

Skingle, Arthur and Sparrow, Peter (1971)

On the evening of 27 June 1971, Detective Constable Ian Coward stopped a car containing two men in Reading on suspicion of drunk driving. As the policeman approached the vehicle, Skingle shot him nine times. Coward died a month later. Skingle had just been released from prison and Sparrow also had a criminal record. Witnesses identified them from mug shots and they were picked up, tried and sentenced to life terms for the murder.

Anarchists hijack a tram in Tottenham; police pursue them in another tram.

Guerin, Joseph (1971)

One evening in 1971, Mike McNeil, a police sergeant in New York, pulled in a car driver whose licence did not match the car's registration number. As he was questioning the man, the other three occupants of the car drove off. McNeil caught them, searched them, then climbed into the driver's seat. Guerin had a concealed revolver and shot McNeil several times in the head. Guerin ran off, but the other occupants remained to give evidence. Guerin had been wanted for robbery and was sentenced to life imprisonment.

The Murder of PC Yvonne Fletcher (1984)

In November 1999, the Libyan government agreed to pay compensation to the family of PC

Yvonne Fletcher. Fletcher was a serving officer murdered outside the Libyan Embassy in London in 1984, whilst on duty at a demonstration against the Libyan leader, Colonel Gaddafi.

The Events

The burst of fire had killed Yvonne Fletcher and injured 11 other people, mostly Libyan dissidents, after which there had been a tense 10-day siege before the 22 Libyan officials had been allowed to leave Britain. The police had been forced to allow the gunman and his accomplices to leave the Libyan Peoples' Bureau and fly to Tripoli because of their diplomatic immunity. To date, no one has been charged for the murder of the policewoman.

A memorial stone for Yvonne Fletcher in St James Square, London.

The Murder of PC Blakelock (1985)

During the Broadwater Farm Riots in Tottenham, London, in 1985, PC Keith Blakelock was hacked to death whilst trying to protect firemen who were dealing with a blaze.

Catching the Killers

In 1987, Winston Silcott, Mark Braithwaite and Engin Raghip were all convicted of his murder, but the convictions were later overturned on appeal; it was felt that the police had fabricated evidence to implicate the three men. Silcott was later awarded punitive damages for the wrongful conviction, but was given a life sentence for the murder of a nightclub bouncer, Anthony Smith. Silcott was released in 2003.

Recent Developments

In 2010, police announced they had arrested another man in connection with the murder of Keith Blakelock. Although he was released on bail, they have said this arrest is 'significant' in the case.

Assassination Organizations

Perhaps more frightening than a lone killer with a grudge against someone in power is a whole group of them. Throughout history, there have been several notorious organizations that have planned the assassinations of famous figures, to create panic and to make a point.

Secret Army Organization (1962–65)

The Secret Army Organization, or the Organisation de l'Armée Secrète, was a right-wing group that decided to take direct action against French moves to give Algeria independence.

Assassination Attempts

They first tried to blow up President Charles de Gaulle in Aube, but the roadside bomb failed to explode. In January 1962, they killed one and wounded 13 when they exploded a bomb in the Foreign Ministry in Paris. On 22 August 1962, they carried out a machine-gun attack on the car carrying de Gaulle in the suburbs of Paris. He escaped unscathed and most of the former French soldiers who had carried out the attack were arrested. They made two more attempts in March 1963 and five more in 1964, followed by three others in 1965.

See Carlos the Jackal p. 26

Baader Meinhof (1968–77)

The Red Army Faction (RAF) was led by Andreas Baader and Ulrike Meinhof and was one of three terrorist groups active in West Germany between 1968 and 1977. At least in principle, the Baader Meinhof gang wished to overthrow capitalist society, yet they had a strange mixture of political ideals that were difficult to determine.

The Trial and Continued Activities

Following the siege of the West German Embassy in Stockholm in April 1975, the bulk of the gang were finally rounded up. They were placed on trial in 1976; it lasted two years, the longest and most expensive trial in West German history. Baader and Meinhof committed suicide in prison along with the other two founders of the group, Gudrun Ensslin and Jan-Karl Raspe. In all, 26 of the group were tried, most receiving long sentences. Even while the main gang leaders were in prison, other members were still active, kidnapping and hijacking in order to make demands for the release of the others. All attempts failed; all they had achieved was to make the West German government more powerful. The group formally ceased operations in 1992. Over the years, they were responsible for a multitude of kidnappings, assassinations, robberies, arson attacks and bombings.

Damage to a department store following an arson attack by Baader Meinhof terrorists.

The Weathermen (1970s)

During US involvement in the Vietnam War, a number of civil rights groups and students were involved in protests against government policy. A group known as the Weathermen was a far more radical faction that planted bombs in its attempt to convince America to change its policies. When America's involvement in the Vietnam War ended, the reason for their existence also stopped. The Weathermen group gave way to a more violent organization with links to the Black Panthers and the Black Liberation Army, who would carry out a series of robberies, including the Brinks robbery in 1981.

Bulgarian Secret Service (1978)

Georgi Markov was a Bulgarian refugee who had fled the authorities and had been granted political asylum in Britain. He began working for the BBC World Service, broadcasting to Bulgaria, and incurred the wrath of those in power there. On 7 September 1978, whilst walking along The Strand, Markov was prodded in the thigh with an umbrella. He had been poisoned with ricin, delivered by a pellet with microscopic holes.

2

multiple murders

Massacres

A massacre is defined as the indiscriminate slaughter of people. They are often political in intent, but sometimes those perpetrating a massacre are simply tyrants wishing to exert their power or oppress a people.

Vlad the Impaler (1400s)

Vlad the Impaler, or Vlad Tepes, was a fifteenth-century Wallachian ruler who, over 400 years later, was immortalized as *Dracula* (*'son of the devil'*) by the author Bram Stoker. During his various dynastic struggles and wars against the Turks and Hungarians, Vlad had tens of thousands of victims impaled on stakes. In 1461 Vlad ordered the massacre of all Turks at Giurgiu; nearly 24,000 perished. When he was captured by the Hungarians in the late 1460s, Vlad spent his time in prison impaling small animals. Vlad would relish having banquets surrounded by impaled victims in agonizing pain; unfaithful women would be skinned alive and other victims would be literally worked to death.

Vlad's end came in January 1477, when his small army was attacked by Turks near Bucharest; his head was conveyed to the Turkish sultan in triumph.

Vlad the Impaler, the fearsome ruler who provided the basis for Bram Stoker's *Dracula*.

Ivan the Terrible (1530-84)

Ivan the Terrible was a sixteenth-century Russian tyrant who used unparalleled savagery to create an empire. As a child, Ivan liked to throw dogs from a castle tower. At 13, he set hunting dogs on a key rival and at 17, during his honeymoon, he set fire to men who interrupted his celebrations. He created a secret police to kill for him and in 1570, he virtually eliminated Novgorod, murdering over 60,000 people. Ivan's life of murder, torture and rape ended in 1584.

The Houndsditch Killings and the Sidney Street Siege (1910)

The Sidney Street Siege, or the Battle of Stepney as it was also known, was the culmination of a series of armed burglaries in the Houndsditch area that had claimed the lives of three policemen.

London police line, Sidney Street in Houndsditch, with shotguns at the ready.

The Siege

The desperados – Latvian and Russian nationals – were cornered in a house in Sidney Street in December 1910 and were besieged until 2 January 1911. Attempts to seek a peaceful resolution were met with a hail of gunfire. At one point, operations were directed by the home secretary, Winston Churchill. Eventually, the revolutionaries set the house on fire. Two bodies were found and four other members of the gang were arrested. It was established that the two dead men had been the Houndsditch killers and the other four were later released.

See The Tottenham Outrage p. 31

Lundgren, Jeffrey (1989)

Jeffrey Lundgren led a small group of around 12 people who broke away from the large establishment, the Reorganized Church of Jesus Christ of Latter Day Saints, in 1987. He claimed that the group was too liberal, but there were suggestions that he had been embezzling money.

Cult Leader

Lundgren set up his new church at Kirtland, Utah, where he enjoyed exclusive rule and gave his followers paramilitary training; there were also rumours of strange sexual rituals. One family, the Averys, opposed Lundgren and he had them thrown into a pit, where he executed them and then buried them. Working from a tip-off, police raided the cult's headquarters and Lundgren was sentenced to death for the murders, whilst his wife and son were given long prison sentences. He was executed in October 2006.

Waco, Texas (1993)

While David Koresh, born Vernon Wayne Howell, believed he was an angel and an agent of God, US authorities saw him as a gun-toting criminal who had physically and sexually abused his own children and those of members of his cult. Koresh led a group called the Branch Davidians in an impressive stronghold near Waco, Texas. He had gained control of the cult through force, in a shoot-out in which the former leader, George Roden, had been wounded.

The Waco Siege

Koresh believed that the end of the world would come when the US Army attacked their Mount Carmel compound; he began stockpiling food, weapons and ammunition. The authorities did indeed come on 28 February 1993 to arrest him for illegally holding firearms and explosives. The siege, which began in a volley of shots from the cultists, claimed four US agents, with a further 16 wounded. The siege continued with a war of words until 19 April, when the FBI began organizing a dawn attack. By noon, the compound was engulfed in flames and Koresh and his 76 remaining followers perished. The debate still rages as to who set the fires, although it seems clear that the wooden buildings were doused in petrol.

See Heaven's Gate p. 42

Branch Davidian survivors leave Federal Court in Waco. Texas.

McVeigh, Timothy (1995)

Timothy McVeigh is one of a rare breed: a domestic, home-born American terrorist. McVeigh was a former US Army veteran, who had served during the first Gulf War and had been decorated for his services. After his military career, however, he became violently disillusioned with the American government and was further outraged by the way in which the Waco siege had been handled in 1993.

The Oklahoma Bombing

Deciding to make a stand against the government, he hired a truck and parked it outside the Alfred P. Murrah Federal Building in Oklahoma City. It was packed with a 3,200 kg (7,000 lb) explosive device, a mixture of ammonium nitrate fertilizer and fuel oil. This was detonated on 19 April 1995, shattering the building and killing 168 people.

Trial and Execution

McVeigh faced federal charges for the murder of eight of the employees; the other deaths came under the jurisdiction of the state of Oklahoma. McVeigh's cohort, Michael Fortier, confessed to his involvement and was the prosecution's star witness; he was sentenced to just 12 years in prison. McVeigh became the first person in over 38 years to be executed by the US federal government when he was given a lethal injection in the federal prison at Terre Haute, Indiana, on 11 June 2001.

See The Weathermen p. 35

Heaven's Gate (1997)

The Heaven's Gate doomsday cult was centred in California and was led by Marshall Herff Applewhite and Bonnie Lu Trusdale Nettles. They believed that a UFO would come to Earth and 'recycle' the population. They also believed that, if the group committed suicide, they would be resurrected, as Jesus had been in the Bible and others in the book of Revelations. They thought the body was only a temporary container for the soul and that extra-terrestrials would bring humanity to a higher level.

Suicide Pact

Over three days in 1997, 39 members of the cult committed suicide. Nettles had already died of cancer in 1985. Applewhite was one of those who committed suicide in preparation for the UFO, which they believed was following the Hale-Bopp comet; at Easter 1997 it was at its closest point to the Earth, undoubtedly signalling the suicides.

See Waco, Texas p. 40

The Tadjena Massacre (1998)

On 9 December 1998, Islamic militants perpetrated a massacre at Tadjena, 200 km (60 miles) to the west of Algiers in Algeria. They slit the throats of 42 people. These attacks, which have recurred with growing frequency, are part of the insurgency difficulties in Algeria. In 1992, the elections were cancelled after the Islamic Salvation Front was poised to win. The army took over and, since then, more than 100,000 people have died in the escalating violence.

See The Erfurt Massacre p. 44

School Massacres

School massacres are one of the most horrific crimes committed. The perpetrators are usually driven by feelings of rage or rejection and, after their massacre, they often turn the gun on themselves, denying the families and communities of their victims the consolation of seeing the due process of law applied.

The École Polytechnique Massacre (1989)

On 6 December 1989, Marc Lépine ran riot through this educational institution in Montreal, Canada, murdering 14 women. Lépine blamed women – feminists in particular – for his failed application to be accepted on to an engineering course. Another motive for the killings was the fact that Lépine's pregnant girlfriend intended to have a termination. Lépine began his slaughter by storming into an engineering class and declaring his hatred of feminists, before opening fire on the women in the room. After his rampage, he calmly committed suicide.

The Dunblane Massacre (1996)

Thomas Hamilton was obsessed with small boys and was a former scout leader whose behaviour had been brought into question. On 13 March 1996, Hamilton stormed into a primary school in Dunblane at Stirling in Scotland and fired over 100 rounds in three minutes. He was well armed, with two pistols, Browning semi-automatics, two revolvers and over 700 cartridges. He claimed the lives of one teacher and 15 small children. Fifteen more children were wounded, as were three other teachers. One of the children was pronounced dead on arrival at hospital. After completing the massacre, Hamilton turned a revolver on himself.

Dr Mick North, father of a Dunblane victim, at the 1996 launch of the 'Gun Control Network' pressure group.

Search for a Motive

Apparently, some form of revenge for his dismissal as a scout leader was Hamilton's motive and, in his own mind, it was the gym, in which he had run a boys' club, that was the focus of his rage. The tragedy prompted the government to impose further restrictions on firearms, particularly since Hamilton possessed the weapons legally.

The Erfurt Massacre (2002)

On 26 April 2002, Robert Steinhäuser, dressed like a Japanese ninja, burst into a school in Erfurt, Germany, and murdered 13 teachers, two students and a police officer. Steinhäuser had recently been expelled from the school for truancy. He chose the day deliberately, as his former classmates were sitting examinations. He burst into a classroom armed with a pump-action shotgun and a pistol and began indiscriminately picking off members of staff. Shooting at anyone who moved, he roamed around the school. The police took around 10 minutes to respond and Steinhäuser killed the first of them to appear. A history teacher managed to push him into one of the classrooms, after ripping the mask he wore from his face. With the police arriving in ever-increasing numbers, Robert turned the gun on himself.

See The École Polytechnique Massacre p. 43

Floral tributes are laid out in memory of the Erfurt Massacre victims.

Spree Killings

Spree killings are those that take place at two or more locations with almost no break in between incidents. The term 'killing spree' has also been applied to events perpetrated seemingly indiscriminately, without careful planning or obvious motive over a longer period.

Bonnie and Clyde (1932-34)

Clyde Barrow was 21 when he met the 19-year-old Bonnie Parker; he already had a criminal record for theft and she had been deserted by her robber husband. The day after they met, Clyde was arrested and sentenced to two years in prison; Bonnie helped him escape, but he was recaptured and sentenced to 14 years. In order to gain freedom, he cut off two of his toes with an axe and was paroled.

The First Murder

Bonnie and Clyde's first murder took place in April 1932; later that year, they raided a petrol station in Texas. Bonnie shot and killed a storekeeper in the same state, then they killed a man to steal his car on Christmas Day 1932.

Ambush and Death

In March 1933 in Missouri, they shot and killed two policemen in a gun battle; a few weeks later, they had to shoot their way out of trouble again, during which Clyde's brother, Buck, was killed. On 23 May 1934, their luck finally ran out when their car was ambushed by six police officers. Over 160 shots were fired into the car and the lives of Bonnie and Clyde came to an end, although their legend lives on.

A 1933 photograph of Bonnie and Clyde, taken by Clyde's brother Buck.

Whitman, Charles (1966)

On 31 July 1966, Charles Whitman stabbed and shot his mother, then killed his wife. The following morning, he continued his killing spree with the murder of a receptionist, after which he headed for an observation tower on the Austin campus of the University of Texas, shooting two more people en route.

The Shooting and the Outcome

In just 96 minutes, Whitman killed 16 people and wounded 30 others before the tower was stormed by police. Whitman died in the ensuing gun battle. His attack had been well planned: he had taken with him several guns, plenty of ammunition, food, a radio and even toilet paper. An autopsy of his body discovered a brain tumour, which may have been the cause of his murderous outburst.

See Washington Snipers p. 51

Evans, Donald Leroy (1970)

When Evans left the US Marines in 1970, he went on a killing spree, slaughtering anyone who crossed his path. After his arrest in Gulfport, Mississippi, for the rape and murder of a 10-year-old, Beatrice Routh, Evans confessed to over 60 killings. In 1993, he was tried, convicted and sentenced to death for the Routh murder, then the Florida courts sentenced him to life in 1995 for the strangling of Ira Jean Smith.

The University of Texas tower, from which Charles Whitman shot his victims.

Search for Evidence

Police authorities found it difficult to amass any clear evidence to link Evans with many of the murders he claimed to have committed, but, circumstantially, he was probably responsible for a large percentage of these unsolved murders. Evans was stabbed to death by fellow Mississippi inmate, Jimmy Mack, in January 1999.

See Timothy McVeigh p. 41

Gretzler, Douglas and Steelman, William (1973)

Douglas Gretzler and William Steelman were spree killers who terrorized the south-west of America during the 1970s. Essentially, they were armed robbers, but they never missed an opportunity to commit murder. They met in Denver, Colorado, in the early 1970s and murdered nine people in Arizona. They then held up a store in Victor, California, during which nine more people were killed, four of them children.

Capture and Sentence

The murderous duo were finally cornered at a hotel in Sacramento, California, in 1973. Gretzler gave himself up, but Steelman had to be tear-gassed out. The Californian courts gave them life, but the courts in Arizona sentenced them to death. Steelman died on death row, but Gretzler was executed on 3 June 1998. Police suspect they had actually killed 30 people in total.

See George Banks p. 48

Carpenter, David (1979-81)

David Carpenter, also known as the 'Trailside Killer', had a history of sex crimes and was a major suspect in the investigation into the Zodiac killings. Between 1979 and 1980 Carpenter murdered four women in the Mount Tamalpais Park area near San Francisco. Between October and November 1980, Carpenter killed another four women, three of them in the space of just one weekend.

Later Murders

His spree continued in March 1981; this time, the girl's boyfriend survived and gave police a good description of their attacker. Carpenter struck again on 1 May. When an ex-girlfriend of his, Heather Scaggs, went missing, police followed the trail to Carpenter and finally arrested him. He was sentenced to death in 1984.

See The Zodiac Killer p. 212

Diaz, Robert (1981)

Diaz was a death-dealing nurse who killed 19 people over a 12-day period in April 1981 at the Perris Community Hospital in California. Police received an anonymous tip-off and found vital medical records missing. Diaz (see opposite, left) was arrested in November, but his trial did not begin until March 1984. In the preceding months, exhumations had confirmed that Diaz had used Lidocaine and morphine to dispatch the patients. On 29 March, he received the death sentence.

Robert Diaz (left), who went on a killing spree in a hospital in 1981.

See Beverley Allitt p. 199

Banks, George (1982)

George Banks, from Wilkes-Barre, Pennsylvania, awoke early on 25 September 1982 and proceeded to slaughter his whole family. His three girlfriends, Regina Clemens, Susan Yuhas and Dorothy Lyons, were shot, followed by his four-year-old son, Bowendy, his one-year-old daughter, Mauitania, then his other daughter, Montanzima.

Continuation of the Spree

He then shot 11-year-old Nancy Lyons and her half-brother, Forarounde Banks, before shooting two neighbours, Jimmy Olsen and Ray Hall. Banks then drove to a former girlfriend's home and killed her, her mother, the son they had together, her brothers and a nephew who happened to be staying with them.

Death Row

After a brief siege, Banks surrendered and was subsequently sentenced to death. His sentence has not been carried out, as appeals continue; in May 2010, a judge declared him incompetent to be executed.

See Lyle and Erik Menendez p. 113

Ryan, Michael (1987)

On 19 August 1987, Michael Ryan stalked the streets of Hungerford, Berkshire, shooting at will. He murdered 16 and wounded 14, eight of whom were seriously injured. Ryan was an unemployed labourer with a love of guns and weapons. He had begun the slaughter across the border in Wiltshire, with the cold-blooded killing of Susan Godfrey; he had then driven into Hungerford on the town's market day in order to find more victims.

Siege and Death

As the firing started, one of the victims, a police officer, Roger Bereton, managed to contact another officer, who called in firearms units and a helicopter. Bereton then died where he lay. After rampaging through the town, Ryan barricaded himself in a school and the police surrounded the buildings with snipers. Negotiators made contact with Ryan, who told them: 'I have killed all those people, but I haven't got the guts to blow my own brains out.' Just after 7 p.m., Ryan found the courage and the police discovered him dead in one of the school's classrooms.

Morning newspapers tell of the Hungerford massacre. 20 August 1987.

Sartin, Robert (1989)

During a 20-minute period on Sunday, 30 April 1989 in Monkseaton, Tyne and Wear, Robert Sartin killed one person and wounded 14 others. Schizophrenic Sartin would later claim to have heard voices in his head compelling him to carry out the attacks. He had been obsessed with the Moors Murders committed by Myra Hindley and Ian Brady, and the poisoner Graham Young. He had also visited Hungerford, the site of Michael Ryan's massacre. Sartin habitually wore black, and liked to be known as Satan.

Plea of Insanity

Sartin was just 22 when he strode around Monkseaton armed with a shotgun, discharging the weapon at anyone he saw. When he stood trial in April 1990, he was deemed 'unfit to plead' and was subsequently confined to a psychiatric unit for an indefinite period.

See Ian Brady, Myra Hindley p. 81

Cunanan, Andrew (1997)

On 29 April 1997, Andrew Cunanan, a member of San Diego's gay community, bludgeoned Jeffrey Trail to death in the apartment of David Madson, a former lover living in Minneapolis. Cunanan killed Madson himself four days later; his body was found with multiple gunshot wounds. In May, he stabbed Lee Miglin to death in Chicago and shot William Rees in New Jersey. On the morning of 15 July, he shot the fashion guru Gianni Versace outside his Miami Beach mansion. There followed a nationwide manhunt that ended when Cunanan's body was found in a houseboat near the Versace murder scene.

See The Station Strangler p. 60

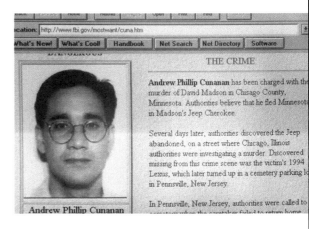

Andrew Cunanan, who murdered fashion designer Gianni Versace in 1997.

Muhammad, John Allen and Malvo, John Lee (2002)

Between 2 and 22 October 2002, the Washington DC, Maryland and Virginia areas of the US were subjected to a series of indiscriminate sniper incidents that sent fear to the hearts of those who lived in the region.

John Allen Muhammad, who was arrested over the DC area sniper attacks in 2002.

Police Hunt and Arrest

After many false leads, John Allen Muhammad and his 17-year-old stepson, John Lee Malvo, were found sleeping in their car and arrested. The two men, who became known as the Washington Snipers, had targeted civilians and had left a tarot card at the scene of one of the shootings, which stated, 'Dear Mr Policeman, I am God'. In a letter left at another scene, the snipers stated, 'Your children are not safe anywhere or any time'. They had demanded $10 million.

Trials and Sentencing

The three states vied for the opportunity to prosecute. In November 2006, Malvo was convicted in Maryland and sentenced to six life sentences without parole. Muhammad faced trials in Maryland and Virginia, and was sentenced to death. He was executed by lethal injection in November 2009.

See Charles Whitman p. 46

Derrick Bird (2010)

On 2 June 2010, Derrick Bird went on a killing spree in Cumbria, murdering 12 people (including his twin brother) and injuring 11 others, before finally killing himself. He began in Lamplugh in mid-morning and moved through other villages, gunning people down at random. Bird, a taxi driver, is thought to have been motivated to such rage by disagreement over a family will.

See The Dunblane Massacre p. 43

Family Murders

Mass murder is not always random and strangers not always the target. Over the years, there have been many cases in which people turn their murderous intentions towards their own families – even their children.

Cotton, Mary Ann (1840s-72)

Mary Ann Cotton murdered her first husband and five children in the 1840s; she then married George Ward, who met a similar fate. She married again, to a man named John Robinson, who also fell victim to Cotton, along with his children. Cotton moved on again and remarried; her new husband's sister was first to go, then her husband Frederick in 1871, followed by two of their children and a lodger. The last child of the marriage succumbed in 1872.

Discovery and Death

All the victims over the years had apparently died from gastric fever, but in fact the cause of death was arsenic poisoning, a fact discovered in 1872 when the latest batch of corpses was exhumed. Cotton was tried for the last four murders, the jury taking only an hour to find her guilty. She was executed by hanging at Durham on 24 March 1873.

See George Banks p. 48

Doss, Nannie (1920-64)

Nannie Doss, of Tulsa, Oklahoma, killed at least 11 people, including five husbands, her own mother, two of her sisters and two of her children.

Arsenic Poisoning

Doss murdered her two children by poisoning them, an event that caused her first husband to flee in fear of his own life. She remarried and poisoned her second husband, and a third in 1952. Two more husbands succumbed to Doss's stewed prunes laced with arsenic; during this time, her sisters and mother faced the same fate.

Suspicions and Sentencing

On the death of her last husband, the doctor demanded an autopsy and contacted the police. The post-mortem clearly showed he had died from arsenic poisoning. Doss confessed to the string of murders and, in 1964, she was sentenced to life imprisonment. She died the following year from leukaemia.

See Belle Gunness p. 134

Nannie Doss with her daughter and granddaughters in Tulsa courthouse, 1931.

Starkweather, Charles (1958)

On 21 January 1958, Charles Starkweather murdered the family of his 14-year-old girlfriend, Caril Ann Fugate – her mother, father and younger sister. The couple then fled and, for the next week, over 1,200 National Guardsmen and police combed Nebraska and Wyoming in search of them. Before he was finally cornered, Starkweather shot or stabbed a further seven people.

Punishment

He claimed that the killings had begun when Caril Ann's parents had made fun of him. Initially, Starkweather claimed Caril Ann was a hostage, but he later changed his story. She was sentenced to life and was released in 1977. Aged 19, Starkweather had a one-way trip to the electric chair in Nebraska on 25 June 1959. He had modelled himself on James Dean and in at least one respect he was correct: they both died young.

See Bonnie and Clyde p. 45

3

Stranglers

Some of the most notorious serial killers have chosen strangulation as the means for dispatching their victims. Often preceded by rape or torture, the perpetrator may use a variety of objects with which to strangle their victim, from a pair of tights to their bare hands.

Christie, John Reginald Halliday (1940-53)

Between 1940 and 1953, 'Reg' Christie murdered eight women. During the Second World War, Christie was a special reserve constable and had a reputation for his authoritarian and officious attitude.

Early Victims

His first two victims, Ruth Fuerst and Muriel Eady, were raped and strangled, then buried in Christie's back garden whilst his wife, Ethel, was away from the house on holiday or visiting relatives. Beryl Evans, a neighbour, turned to Christie for an abortion in 1949; he battered, strangled and raped her, before killing her baby daughter, Geraldine. Surprisingly, Beryl's husband Timothy confessed to the murders and was hanged in 1950, but he received a posthumous pardon when the evidence against Christie came to light.

Later Victims

In January 1950, prostitutes Rita Nelson and Kathleen Maloney fell victim to Christie, who hid their bodies in a cupboard. By March of the same year, the cupboard also contained the body of Hectorina McLennan. After Christie's sister-in-law informed the police that she had not heard from Ethel, his home at 10 Rillington Place was searched and her body was found buried in the back garden. Christie was charged with her murder and later confessed to the seven other killings. He was hanged on 15 July 1953.

See Hanging p. 247

De Salvo, Albert (1962-64)

De Salvo stalked the streets of Boston between June 1962 and January 1964, claiming at least 13 victims – all women who he raped or sexually assaulted, then strangled, bludgeoned or stabbed. He became known as the 'Boston Strangler'. In December 1962, a psychological profile described him as being of Spanish or Italian origin, of average height, a schizophrenic and probably a mother-hater. Many of his early victims were mature or elderly women, but four of them were either in their late teens or early twenties. He gained entry to women's homes by posing as a workman or policeman.

Albert de Salvo is recaptured by police after escaping from a mental hospital.

The Boston Strangler

On 27 October 1964, De Salvo sexually assaulted a woman he may have intended as his fourteenth murder victim. Inexplicably, he left her alive. Her description of him prompted other women to identify De Salvo as their attacker. While he was being held on a rape charge in 1965, he confessed that he was the Boston Strangler. With no physical evidence to link him to the killings, he never stood trial for any of the crimes but was imprisoned for life for robberies and rapes. He was found murdered in his cell on 26 November 1973.

See Kenneth Bianchi and Angelo Buono p. 58

Carlton, Gary (1977-78)

Gary Carlton was responsible for a series of rapes and murders of elderly women; he became known as the 'Stocking Strangler' due to his method of murder. His murderous career began in September 1977 and continued until April 1978.

Capture and Trial

Carlton was identified by a witness and, as he had already served a prison sentence for the rape of an elderly woman in New York, the police in Columbus, Georgia, were convinced they had the right man. He disappeared until May 1984, when he was finally picked up in Atlanta and charged with the murder, rape and robbery of three women. He was found guilty of murder and sentenced to death; he remains on death row in Jackson, Georgia. There continues to be a lingering doubt as to whether he committed all the Stocking Strangler killings.

Bianchi, Kenneth and Buono, Angelo (1977-79)

The Hillside Strangler was, in fact, two men – cousins Kenneth Bianchi and Angelo Buono. Between 1977 and 1979, seven abductions, rapes and murders took place in Los Angeles that were later linked to the men. Bianchi had been interviewed following this spate of murders, but no proof was found of his involvement.

opening remarks in the murder trial Monday of Angelo Buono, accused in the so-called "Hillside Stranglings" case in Los Angeles. Behind Boren are photos of the 10 women and girls Buono is accused of killing. (AP Laserphoto)(jas21700 pool)1982 SLUG/ Hillside Strangler

Roger Boren, Deputy Attorney General of California, during Angelo Buono's trial.

The Bellingham Murders

When the bodies of Diane Wilder and Karen Mandic were discovered in Bellingham, Washington, in January 1979, his name came up again. The police found forensic evidence, Mandic's telephone number and other incriminating evidence in Bianchi's home. He implicated Buono after he had been arrested and interrogated; it was confirmed that they had carried out the murders together. Buono was convicted of just one of the murders and sentenced to life imprisonment, while Bianchi received multiple life sentences and was imprisoned in Washington.

See Albert De Salvo p. 57

Gacy Jr, John Wayne (1978)

This Chicago-born murderer lured boys into his home, raped and strangled them, then buried their bodies around his swimming pool and under his house, pouring lime over them to assist decomposition. Gacy, who suffered from blackouts after a childhood head injury, murdered 36 youths. His arrest in 1978 came as the result of an assignation with Robert Priest, whose mother reported him missing, informing the police of Robert's meeting with Gacy; they searched his house and discovered a trap door leading to the mass graves. Gacy, who had visited hospitals as 'Pogo the Clown', confessed, but did not testify at his trial. On 13 March 1980, he was sentenced to death and was executed by lethal injection.

See William Bonin and Vernon Butts p. 72

Lopez, Pedro Armando (1980)

Pedro Lopez was the seventh son of a Colombian prostitute. At the age of 18, he had been raped while in prison serving a sentence for car theft. Within days, he had murdered three of the rapists. On his release, Lopez travelled widely throughout Colombia, Ecuador and Peru, largely without companions. He claimed the lives of 100 young girls. He nearly met his end in northern Peru when an Indian tribe caught him trying to make off with a nine-year-old girl. They tortured him and began to bury him alive, but the timely arrival of an American missionary saved him.

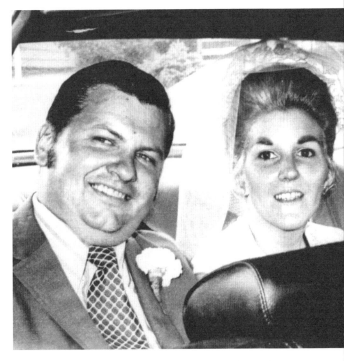

John Wayne Gacy Jr after the wedding to his second wife, Carole Hoff, in 1972.

Lopez's Confession

In April 1980, a river swollen by rain revealed the bodies of four of his victims near Ambato, Peru. Lopez had recently abducted, raped and murdered another local girl and, this time, the police had a description. Lopez confessed to the abduction, rape and strangulation of at least 300 young girls over a considerable period of time. He was ultimately tried for multiple murders in Ecuador, where he was sentenced to life. The reign of terror of the 'Monster of the Andes' was finally over.

Ridgway, Gary Leon (1983–2001)

On 30 November 2001, Gary Ridgway was arrested for the notorious Green River Killings. He had become a suspect as early as 1983 and in 1987, had given samples that would later link him, via DNA, to the crimes.

The Green River Murders

In the 1980s, the Green River Killer may have murdered up to 50 people in Seattle, Tacoma, Washington and, perhaps, Portland in Oregon. The majority of the victims were prostitutes or runaway teenagers, who had been picked up around the Pacific Highway South. They had all been strangled and dumped near the Green River in the state of Washington. Twenty years later, Ridgway was finally arrested and, after much legal wrangling, he was sentenced to 48 life sentences with no possibility of parole. Ridgway escaped the death penalty because he agreed to give details of the murders.

See Robert Black p. 82

The Station Strangler (1986–94)

Between 1986 and 1994, 21 mixed-race boys and young men were raped, strangled and buried in shallow graves in the Cape Town area of South Africa. The alleged killer is Norman Afzal Simons, who was given a 25-year sentence in 1994 for the murder of a 10-year-old boy, whom he had abducted from Cape Town's Strand Station; the body was found 10 days later.

Simons' Denial

Although Simons has never admitted to the sex killings, he related the reason for killing the child to when he was raped by his own brother as a young boy. He claimed that, when his brother was murdered in 1991, his spirit entered him and ordered him to rape and kill. Serial killer profilers are convinced that Simons is the Station Strangler.

Graham, Harrison (1987)

Harrison Graham was a rather slow-witted man from Philadelphia, but he appears to have been fairly well liked. Eventually, however, neighbours complained to the landlord about the rank smells emanating from his apartment. Graham argued with the landlord, which resulted in his eviction; he made sure he had nailed the bedroom door shut before leaving, claiming his valuables were inside.

Six Death Penalties

On 9 August 1987, the landlord called the police to break down the door; inside were the decomposing corpses of seven women. Graham claimed they had been there when he moved in, but forensics showed they had been strangled, then abused after death by

Harrison Graham smiles and gestures as he leaves court after being found guilty.

Graham. He was found guilty on all counts and sentenced to life and six electrocutions – after serving his full sentence, he will be electrocuted.

See Crime Scene Science p. 234

Gun Murders

Gun crime is widespread, particularly in countries that allow the legal possession of firearms. Some of the worst serial killers of the last century have used guns as their weapon of choice when carrying out their murderous sprees.

Mullin, Herb (1972-73)

Herb Mullin came from a religious background and appears to have become mentally unbalanced following the death of his best friend, Dean Richardson, in a car accident in July 1965. Mullin created a shrine to Dean in his bedroom, broke off his engagement, claimed he was homosexual and declared he was a conscientious objector when he was called up in 1969. Hallucinogenic drugs fuelled his paranoid schizophrenia.

Paranoia Turns to Murder

Mullin committed his first murder in October 1972, beating a tramp to death with a baseball bat. Eleven days later, he stabbed a college student and disembowelled her, leaving her body for the vultures. In January 1973, he shot five people, and a further four the following month. He was soon captured and found guilty of 10 murders; he will be eligible for parole in 2025.

Berkowitz, David (1975-77)

Adopted at birth by a Jewish couple, Nat and Pearl Berkowitz, David was something of a loner as a child. The death of his adopted mother affected him badly and he made his first bungled attempt at murdering a woman on 24 December 1975. Seven months later, he bought a handgun and approached a car containing two women. He fired through the windscreen, killing Donna Laurie and wounding Jodi Valenti. He then set out on nightly hunts for new victims.

Son of Sam

His second successful attack came on 23 October 1976, when he mistakenly shot Carl DeNaro, a long-haired male, but just a month later, he shot Donna DeMasi and Joanne Lomino dead while they were seated on their porch. Christine Freund fell victim on 30 January 1977 and, in March, Virginia Voskerichian, then Valentina Suriani and Alexander Esau in April, when Berkowitz wrote a note to the police, signing himself 'Son of Sam'.

Four of the six women killed by 'Son of Sam' David Berkowitz.

End of the Reign of Terror

He killed again on 31 July 1977, but this time was to be his last. He was arrested and, after psychiatric tests, considered fit to stand trial, where he pleaded guilty. He received 547 years and served his sentence in Attica Prison, in the Catskill Mountains, New York.

See Forensic Handwriting p. 243

Onoprienko, Anatoly (1989-96)

On 16 April 1996, Anatoly Onoprienko was arrested at his girlfriend's home in the Ukraine, thus ending the career of the killer known as the 'Terminator', who may have claimed as many as 52 lives. Initially, he admitted to eight killings between 1989 and 1995. In 1996 alone, it is believed that he slaughtered eight entire families.

Motives for the Terminator

His motives are confused, although certainly he robbed his victims; he would gun down adults and batter children to death; his preferred weapon was a shotgun. During his trial, he never expressed any regrets and openly confessed to many of the killings. In March 1997, the Ukrainian court sentenced him to death, although to date there is still a moratorium on executions. Onoprienko himself wishes to be killed, warning that if he were ever released, he would kill until killed.

See Andrei Romanovich Chikatilo p. 67

Cannibalism and Mutilation

Many serial killers are not satisfied with simple murder. They kill to fulfil sinister needs and fantasies. Some are 'vampires' – drinking their victims' blood. Others indulge in cannibalistic practices. Still others find ways of mutilating their victims, before or after death.

The Sawney Bean Family (1600s)

The Sawney Bean family lived in Ayrshire in Scotland perhaps as far back as the seventeenth century. They lived in a cave complex and were robbers and cannibals. The family were certainly active over two decades, interbreeding until they had created a small army. A 400-strong force, with tracker dogs and supported by local volunteers, were sent to root out the cannibals. They found the cave, with human meat hung up as in a butcher's shop. The family was overpowered and taken back to Edinburgh. The 27 Sawney Bean men had their limbs cut off and were bled to death in front of the women, after which the 21 women were burned alive on pyres.

See Vlad the Impaler p. 38

Gein, Eddie (1954)

Eddie Gein lived in Wisconsin, USA. Following the deaths of his father and brother, he lived with his strictly Lutheran mother, Augusta, as a virtual recluse on their family farmstead. When his mother died in December 1945, the lonely, eccentric bachelor Eddie Gein found it impossible to bear. He skinned her body and tanned the flesh, wearing it and her clothes in an attempt to reincarnate her. He then began robbing graves and taking the bodies home to preserve them, before finally turning to murder.

Gein's Victims

Mary Hogan was Gein's first known victim in 1954, followed by Bernice Worden. When Worden's son found a receipt from their hardware store in Bernice's handwriting made out to Gein, the killer was charged with and confessed to the two murders, but insufficient evidence linked him with the skin and body parts of a further 15 women that were found around his home. Gein was deemed to be insane and committed to an institution, where he died in 1984.

See Jeffrey Dahmer p. 67

Kearney, Patrick Wayne (1975-77)

Eddie Gein, the model for numerous cinematic psychos, including Leatherface and Norman Bates.

Patrick Kearney and his lover David D. Hill killed and dismembered at least 28 male victims between 1975 and 1977. The two men were army veterans and lived in a meticulously kept bachelor apartment in Redondo Beach, California.

The Trash-Bag Killers

With Kearney taking the lead, they committed a series of killings known as the 'Trash-Bag Murders', as the dismembered corpses were found dumped along Californian highways in black bin bags. The couple surrendered in July 1977 after seeing a wanted poster of themselves and knowing that they would inevitably be caught. Hill was released due to lack of evidence, but Kearney was sentenced to multiple life imprisonment. He explained that the killings excited him and made him feel dominant.

See Juan Corona p. 70

Nilsen, Dennis (1978-83)

Civil servant Dennis Nilsen turned two of his homes, in London and Cricklewood, into slaughterhouses in which he claimed at least 29 lives between 1978 and 1983.

Hiding the Bodies

Nilsen, a homosexual, picked up young men in central London and murdered them, then dismembered their bodies. His primary problem was the disposal of the corpses, which he either kept in bags in his home, hidden under floorboards, or attempted to flush down the lavatory. When manholes were checked to discover the source of a foul stench at his Cranley Gardens home in February 1983, lumps of human flesh were discovered.

The pot and stove used by Dennis Nilsen to boil the severed heads of his victims.

Nilsen's Confession

At first, he denied knowledge of the bodies, but under questioning later, he made a full confession, detailing at length all his murders. Over the course of 11 days, Nilsen dictated some 30 hours of confessions, describing how he had picked up mainly vagrants and extracted sexual favours from them in exchange for food and shelter. His abiding desire, having established a relationship of sorts with the men, was that they should never leave him. Nilsen stood trial in October 1983 and was found both sane and guilty of the six specimen murder charges and two attempted murders. He was sentenced to life imprisonment.

See Ted Bundy p. 71

Chikatilo, Andrei Romanovich (1978-90)

Between 1978 and 1990, the 'Rostov Ripper', or the 'Forest-Strip Killer', claimed at least 55 young lives in Russia. The Ripper, Andrei Chikatilo, was a schoolteacher and grandfather who preyed on the homeless and solitary children. He would lure them into woodland, cut out their tongues, gouge out their eyes and perforate their eardrums before raping, mutilating and cannibalizing the victims.

Capture and Execution

Chikatilo had been picked up in connection with the crimes in both 1979 and 1984. On the second occasion, he had been blood-tested, but his group did not match samples found at the murder scenes. In some rare cases, blood, semen or saliva from the same individual can be from different serological groups. Chikatilo was finally arrested after surveillance in November 1990 and in February 1994 he was executed.

See Serology p. 239

Dahmer, Jeffrey (1978-91)

Jeffrey Dahmer, the 'Milwaukee Cannibal', is undoubtedly one of the most terrifying and gruesome of all serial killers. Between 1978 and 1991, Dahmer may have murdered as many as 17 young men.

The Milwaukee Cannibal

He was a depraved psychopath, cannibal and necrophile, who already had convictions for child molesting. He would invite young men back to his apartment, drug them, handcuff them and then either strangle or stab them to death. In other instances, he would carry out his own medical experiments, including attempts to lobotomize his victims, or drill holes in their skulls and pour in acid. Once the victim was dead, he would dismember the corpse and keep parts of their bodies either pickled or frozen as trophies.

Uncovering the Evidence

When Dahmer was arrested in July 1991, following a lead from Tracy Edwards, a young man who had managed to escape from Dahmer, the police made innumerable horrific discoveries in his apartment. There were photographs of dismembered bodies, human skulls in the refrigerator, pickled body parts and clear signs that Dahmer had eaten parts of the bodies. Dahmer was sentenced to 957 years, but he was battered to death by a fellow inmate during a prison riot in November 1994.

See Juan Corona p. 70

Dzhumagaliev, Nikolai (1980-89)

Despite his strange, metal false teeth, Nikolai Dzhumagaliev was a hit with women; they never suspected his evil desires to rape them and hack them to pieces with an axe. Dzhumagaliev had already served a prison sentence for manslaughter in Khazakstan in 1980, but now he was loose in Moscow.

Jeffrey Dahmer appears in Milwaukee County Circuit Court in 1991.

A Gruesome Discovery

Dzhumagaliev was a cannibal and it was this habit that brought about his downfall. When two friends were invited for a meal, they discovered the severed head of a woman. They contacted the police and Dzhumagaliev was arrested. He was convicted of seven murders and confined to a mental institution.

Sexually Motivated Murders

Sex, or lust killers, are driven by sexual desires, often fuelled by repression or a need for gratification. In most cases, the victim is raped before being killed, and the murderer's fantasies play a large part in their rituals.

Glatman, Harvey (1957–59)

Harvey Glatman had been an odd child and, as he grew older, his sexual activity took to extremes that bordered on hanging himself. In 1945, armed with a cap-gun, he attempted to make a girl undress, for which he was caught and arrested. Breaking bail, he fled to New York, but was arrested again and imprisoned for robbery.

Glatman's Victims

After his release in 1951, he moved to Los Angeles, living a life of a near-recluse. In 1957, he began recruiting women to accept nude-modelling photographic assignments. His first victim, Judy Dull, was repeatedly raped, then strangled and buried. In March 1958 he claimed a second victim, Shirley Bridgeford, whose body was abandoned in a desert near San Diego. In July, he murdered Ruth Mercado.

Harvey Glatman, a serial rapist and strangler.

Downfall and Death

His downfall came after a desperate struggle with intended victim Lorraine Vigil; a policeman intervened and arrested Glatman. He confessed and was executed in the gas chamber at San Quentin in August 1959.

See Ian Brady and Myra Hindley p. 81

Moseley, Winston (1964)

Winston Moseley was arrested in March 1964; he had no criminal record but he had committed innumerable burglaries, dozens of rapes and at least three murders. In 1964, he had been picked up literally in the act of murdering Kitty Genovese in New York, and immediately made a confession.

Release Attempts

In 1968, having been found guilty and sentenced to death – later commuted to life imprisonment – he escaped from the hospital where he was being held and took five people hostage, during which time he committed a rape. He was returned to prison after surrendering. In recent years he has attempted to secure his release after nearly four decades in prison. He is next eligible for parole in 2011. Undoubtedly, Moseley is a psychopath and whether he has truly been rehabilitated is uncertain.

Corona, Juan (1971)

Corona was born in Mexico but moved to California in the 1950s. Both he and his brother, Natividad, were homosexual with homicidal tendencies. Natividad had attacked a man in a café in 1970 with a machete. The true scope of their crimes – for which Juan would subsequently receive 25 life sentences – began before May 1971.

The Start of the Spree

Juan had been working as a contract labourer in an orchard in California. The orchard-owner discovered a fresh grave and contacted the authorities; it contained the body of Kenneth Whittaker, who had been stabbed and his skull torn open with a sharp object, possibly a machete. After nine days of intensive searching, investigators discovered 25 graves; in each of these, they found the heavily mutilated bodies of migrant workers, alcoholics and drifters, none of whom had been reported missing. All showed signs of homosexual rape. Juan had foolishly left receipts containing his signature in two of the graves. Nonetheless, it took the jury 45 hours to convict him on all murder counts. Juan's defence lawyers had tried to place the blame upon Nativadad.

See Patrick Wayne Kearney p. 65 Juan Corona arrives at Yuba City courthouse in 1971.

Bundy, Theodore (Ted) Robert (1972-78)

Bundy was a highly educated man, handsome and attractive to women. In the period up to 1972, there were several of killings of young women in the Washington State area, which abruptly stopped when Bundy moved to the University of Utah in Salt Lake. A new epidemic of murders broke out there.

Extradition and Escape

In 1977, Bundy was arrested for the kidnapping of Carol DaRonch and was then linked to the earlier killing of Caryn Campbell. Bundy was extradited to Colorado to face the Campbell murder charge, but he escaped in June. He was quickly recaptured, but escaped again six months later and carried out another series of murders, rapes and robberies in Florida.

Ted Bundy, who eventually confessed to over 100 murders.

Chance Recapture

Bundy was to remain at large until February 1978, when he was picked up by chance for a minor traffic offence. It was then, under interrogation, that he admitted to over 100 killings. At his subsequent trial, Bundy was sentenced to death, but made repeated appeals and assisted the FBI in constructing psychological profiles of serial killers. Psychological profiles of Bundy himself revealed few clues as to why he became a serial killer. In his own words, 'sometimes I feel like a vampire'. He was executed on 24 January 1989.

See Richard Ramirez p. 91

Bonin, William and Butts, Vernon (1972–80)

William Bonin and Vernon Butts murdered 41 young men between 1972 and 1980, raping, then strangling and, in some cases, mutilating their bodies. The series of murders, known as the 'Freeway Killings', took place across southern California. The police linked the convicted rapist Bonin with the attacks and put him under surveillance, catching him in the act in June 1980.

Death of the Freeway Killers

He implicated Vernon Butts and later James Monro and Gregory Miley. Butts committed suicide in prison in January 1981; Miley provided evidence against Bonin, who was convicted of the rape, torture and murder of 10 of his victims and executed by lethal injection on 23 February 1996. Bonin's and Butts' victims had mainly been young male hitchhikers. Bonin said, 'I'd still be killing, I couldn't stop killing'.

See Patrick Wayne Kearney p. 65

Gallego, Gerald and Williams-Gallego, Charlene (1978-80)

In rare cases, murder runs in the family. Gerald Gallego's father had been executed in Mississippi for the murder of a prison guard, but Gerald eclipsed his father's notoriety. Together with his seventh wife, Charlene, he embarked on a series of kidnappings, rapes and murders – targeting female hitchhikers – throughout California and Nevada, claiming at least 10 lives.

Results of the Manhunt

After an intensive manhunt, Gerald and Charlene surrendered to the police in Omaha, Nebraska, and were extradited to California. There, Gerald was convicted of the murders and sentenced to death. The couple were then again extradited, to Nevada, with Charlene making a full confession, as she had done in California. Gerald was found guilty and sentenced to death by means of a lethal injection, whilst Charlene was given 16 years imprisonment.

See Paul Bernardo and Carla Homolka p. 75

Clark, Douglas and Bundy, Carol (1980)

Douglas Clark used his cohort Carol Bundy to convince girls to get into their car. Clark was a necrophile and whilst raping the girls, he would shoot them in the head. He also kept the heads as trophies and for further abuse. Clark killed Gina Marano, Cynthia Chandler, Exxie Wilson and Karen Jones in June 1980. Clark became known as the Sunset Strip Killer, as all his murders took place around the Hollywood area. The last victim was a friend of Bundy's, John

Murray, in whom she had confided. Bundy finally turned Clark over to the police; she was sentenced to two life sentences and Clark was sent to the gas chamber.

See Ian Brady and Myra Hindley p. 81

Georges, Guy (1991–97)

Between 1991 and 1997, the vagrant Guy Georges tortured, raped and murdered seven women in the area around the Bastille in Paris. Georges would ingratiate himself with his intended victim, gaining an invitation to their homes, where he would torture and rape them and slit their throats. Georges' DNA had been on file for three years before he was arrested. He had been questioned about three rapes and murders that had been committed between 1991 and 1994. When he came to trial in March 2001, he was described as a narcissistic psychopath, but initially denied the charges. On 5 April, he confessed and was sentenced to life imprisonment with no parole for at least 22 years.

See DNA Testing p. 238

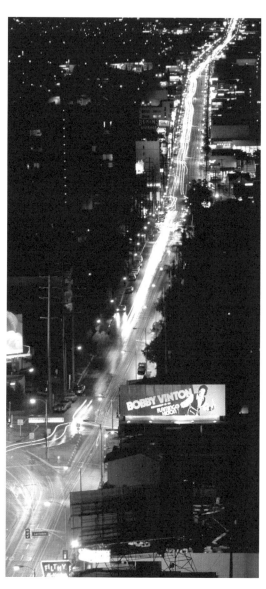

Sunset Strip in Los Angeles, where Douglas Clark laid siege in the summer of 1980.

Bernardo, Paul and Homolka, Carla (1990–92)

Husband and wife serial killers Paul and Carla Bernado were known as Ken and Barbie by their neighbours in Canada, but they were responsible for 43 sexual attacks and a string of murders, many of which they filmed.

A Marriage of Murderers

Possibly motivated by the fact that Carla was not a virgin when they married, Paul demanded his wife's assistance in taking the virginity of her younger sister, Tammy. In a botched attempt to anaesthetize her so that Paul could rape her, Tammy choked on her own vomit. Carla began to procure women for Paul's unbridled sexual appetite. The couple killed three people in all and became Canada's most notorious modern-day criminals. DNA from the string of rapes linked Bernardo to the killings, and when police found the couple's tapes, it was enough to sentence them both to life imprisonment.

See Gerald Gallego and Charlene Williams-Gallego p. 73

Resendez, Angel (1997–99)

Resendez became known as the 'Railway Killer', because his crimes took place near railroad tracks in three states in America. He became the subject of an international manhunt for the murder of nine women, who he had beaten, stabbed and sexually assaulted. Resendez gave himself up in El Paso, Texas.

The Railway Killer

Resendez, who was known throughout much of the manhunt by his alias of Rafael Ramirez, claimed his first victim in 1997 and systematically used the railroad to move in and out of areas, to avoid detection and to be close to potential victims, until June 1999. Resendez finally turned himself in and was convicted of seven killings. He was sentenced to death but still remains in prison as he gradually exhausts the appeal process.

See Juan Corona p. 70

Prostitute Murders

The most notorious prostitute killer is of course Jack the Ripper, but since his time, many serial killers have targeted street women. Sometimes, this is simply because they are seen to be easy victims, but in other cases, the murderer believes he is 'cleaning up' the streets and ridding the world of a particular evil.

Cole, Carroll Edward (1971–81)

Between 1971 and 1981, Cole murdered 35 women. His victims were what he described as 'loose women'; his motive being that they reminded him of his mother.

First Victims

In San Diego in 1971, he strangled Essie Louie Buck; in Las Vegas in 1977, he strangled Kathlyn Blum. He dodged between San Diego, Las Vegas and Dallas from 1979 to 1980, strangling Marnie Cushman, Bonnie O'Neil, Dorothy King and Wanda Faye Roberts. In most of the cases, Cole had sexually abused the bodies after death. In November 1980, he strangled Sally Thompson, but neighbours called the police to investigate the noise. Incredibly, Cole was released before being re-arrested and subsequently confessing to the murders.

Trial and Execution

A Texas court tried him on three counts of homicide in April 1981; he confessed to having killed in Oklahoma, Texas, Nevada, California and Wyoming. He pleaded insanity on the basis that he had cannibalized one of his victims. The court was unconvinced and sentenced him to three life terms. Cole then faced trial in Nevada for two murders; again, he pleaded guilty and he asked for the death sentence to be imposed; they duly obliged and Cole was executed by lethal injection on 6 December 1985.

Sutcliffe, Peter (1976-81)

At the time, the infamous 'Yorkshire Ripper' case was the largest manhunt ever launched in Britain – some 250,000 people were interviewed and over 30,000 statements made.

The Yorkshire Ripper

For over five years, the Yorkshire Ripper preyed on lone women, many of whom were prostitutes. On several occasions, former grave digger Peter Sutcliffe had been interviewed, but he had not been directly linked to the brutal attacks and murders. Sutcliffe would later admit to 20 attacks, using a hammer to incapacitate his victims before he stabbed and mutilated them. Thirteen women died from the assaults. Hoax letters and an audio tape supposedly from the Ripper confused the police and, for a time, directed them away from Sutcliffe.

Detectives discover yet another Yorkshire Ripper victim.

Chance Capture

It was pure chance, rather than investigative techniques, which led to Sutcliffe's capture on 2 January 1981. A routine police check on a parked car at night revealed Peter Williams, Sutcliffe's cover name. He confessed to the murders under questioning and claimed he had been told by God to rid the streets of prostitutes. On 22 May 1981 he was found guilty of 13 murders and sentenced to a minimum of 30 years imprisonment.

See Jack the Ripper p. 208

Armstrong, John Eric (1992-2000)

John Eric Armstrong, one of the most travelled serial killers in criminal history, was a member of the US Navy. Between 1992 and 1999, he was responsible for prostitute murders in countries as far afield as Hong Kong, Israel, Korea, Singapore and Thailand, as well as in his homeland of the United States. Following a prostitute murder in Detroit, Armstrong himself called the police; they were sceptical of the 'law-abiding' citizen's explanations and began keeping him under surveillance. The police found the bodies of the victims near railway tracks in Detroit and, working on a serial-killer profile, realized Armstrong would return to bury another body there. Armstrong returned on 12 April 2000 and, since then, police have been trying to link his confessions to a string of murders across the world.

The front door of the house where Kendall Francois lived and stored his victims' corpses.

Francois, Kendall (1996-98)

Between October 1996 and the early months of the following year, three New York prostitutes disappeared without a trace. In March 1997, another was reported missing, then a fifth. Fear for Mary Giaccone's life came when she failed to attend her mother's funeral in the November.

The Victims' Similarities

All the women closely resembled one another – they were all short, petite and with brown hair and blue eyes. Sandra Dean French's car was discovered just a short distance from Francois' home in June 1998, then in August, Catina Newmaster similarly disappeared. On 1 September, Francois was picked up for assaulting a woman. Under interrogation, he admitted to being responsible for the disappearances. When the police searched his home, they made the shocking discovery of eight putrefying corpses. Francois pleaded guilty in court and was sentenced to life imprisonment without the possibility of parole. He had contracted HIV from one of his victims.

Hanaei, Saeed (2000-01)

Hanaei turned to murder after a man propositioned his wife, believing her to be a prostitute. Hanaei embarked on his own personal crusade to clean up the streets of the Iranian city of Mashhad; he was to become known as the 'Spider Killer'.

The Spider Killer

Between 2000 and his capture in July 2001, Hanaei strangled 16 women with their own headscarves and dumped their bodies. He posed as a customer, sexually assaulted the women, then killed them. He admitted to the murders and was hanged before his relatives on 16 April 2002. Three other similar murders in the city, at first attributed to Hanaei, were later proved to have been committed by copy-cat killers. At the time, Hanaei was hailed as an Islamic hero as he 'did not spill the blood of innocents'.

Child Killers

Nothing shocks the public so much as attacks on children, and the serial murder of innocents seems the worst crime of all. Those who kill children may have been abused as children themselves, or they may have paedophiliac tendencies.

Hatcher, Charles (1961-81)

Hatcher was already serving a sentence for abducting a newspaper boy when he committed his first recorded murder in prison in 1961; lack of evidence saved him from prosecution. He was released in 1969 and in August, he abducted and strangled a 12-year-old boy. Later in the month, he was arrested for raping a five-year-old in San Francisco. Hatcher was released on licence in 1977. In May 1978, he murdered a four-year-old child, and was arrested the following year for attempted murder; he was confined in a secure hospital for a year. In June 1981, he stabbed a man to death in Illinois and then murdered an 11-year-old girl in July 1982. Hatcher was again arrested and confessed to three murders.

Hatcher's Suicide

He pleaded guilty to one of the murders in court in October 1982 and was found guilty of another in September 1984. Hatcher committed suicide in prison on 7 December 1984. Over the period 1961 to 1982, Hatcher had committed at least 16 sex-related murders.

See The Station Strangler p. 60

Gonzales, Delfina and Jesus, Maria de (1963-64)

Over a 10-year period, these Mexican sisters claimed the lives of over 80 girls. Delfina and Maria ran a brothel at their Rancho El Angel, staffed by abducted girls forced into drug dependency. If the girls caused problems or lost their appeal, the sisters killed them.

Police Suspicions

In 1964, a woman named Josefina Guttierez was picked up by the Mexican police. She told them of her procurement of girls for the Gonzales sisters and their brothel near San Francisco del Rincon. The police mounted a raid – they found dormitories full of prostitutes and, in the grounds, the graves of over 80 women. The police also discovered innumerable aborted foetuses, the product of crude operations carried out by the Gonzales sisters. The police found other corpses too; those of some of the clients, migrant workers returning from the United States with significant cash. Inexplicably, for the abduction, enslavement, appalling treatment and eventual murder of the 80 or more victims of their business, the Gonzales sisters were sentenced to just 40 years.

See Fred and Rosemary West p. 87

Brady, Ian and Hindley, Myra (1963–64)

Manchester lovers Brady and Hindley became known as the 'Moors Murderers'. Brady was a sadist, Nazi and pornography-lover when he met Hindley and the couple soon began a cruel campaign of child-abduction, using Hindley's grandmother's home in Wardle Brook Avenue, Hattersley as their base.

The Moors Murders

Among their victims were John Kilbride, who had disappeared in Ashton-under-Lyne in November 1963, and Lesley Ann Downey, who disappeared on Boxing Day 1964. Hindley's brother-in-law, who Brady had been grooming as an accomplice, witnessed Brady's brutal murder of Edward Evans on the night of 6 October 1965. The next day, he reported it to the police and Brady and Hindley were arrested. On 16 October 1965 Lesley Ann's body was discovered in a shallow grave on the moors; the investigating team had managed to locate her grave from photographic evidence showing Hindley crouching in the exact spot. Although police were unconvinced that John and Lesley Ann were the couple's only victims, Brady and Hindley were sent to trial at Chester Assizes in 1966. Brady was found guilty of three murders, and Hindley of two; both were sentenced to life.

Confessions

In 1987, Hindley confessed to the additional murders of Pauline Reade (12 July 1963) and Keith Bennett (16 June 1964), and Brady confirmed her confession. Despite numerous appeals for release, Hindley died in prison in 2003 and Brady remains in Ashworth Special Hospital in Merseyside.

See Charles Manson p. 86

Ian Brady and Myra Hindley, who were imprisoned for life in 1966.

Black, Robert (1982-90)

From 1982 until 1990, thousands of police hours were expended on tracking down a balding, bearded kidnapper, sex offender and murderer. Robert Black's luck ran out in July 1990, when he attempted to abduct a six-year-old girl from Stow on the Scottish border. He was arrested when a sharp-eyed witness who had reported the kidnapping spotted the van for a second time.

Gathering Evidence

Black worked as a delivery van driver and the police could place him in and around the scenes of all the offences through petrol bills and cash withdrawals. Black was charged with the murder, kidnapping and illegal dumping of the bodies of Susan Maxwell (1982), Caroline Hogg (1982) and Sarah Harper (1986). On 19 May 1994, the jury found him guilty on all charges and he was jailed for a minimum of 35 years.

See Gary Leon Ridgway p. 60

Coleman, Alton and Brown, Debra (1984)

Reminiscent of the Moors Murderers, Alton Coleman used Debra Brown to allay the fears of the young girls he

Robert Black is led away after the verdict at Newcastle Crown Court.

intended to rape and murder. The mass murders began in the summer of 1984 with the death of Vernita Wheat, aged nine, who they abducted from Waukegan in Illinois. The couple then abducted two girls from Gary, Illinois, but one survived and gave a description of Coleman. This was followed by the discovery of the body of Donna Williams on 11 July and, shortly after that, of Virginia Temple in Detroit. The couple then murdered Tonnie Storey, Harry and Marlene Waters and Eugene Scott in Ohio. They were recognized and picked up in Chicago; Ohio gave them two death sentences, as did Illinois and Indiana. Coleman was executed by lethal injection in Ohio on 26 April 2002.

Indiscriminate Murders

Not all serial killers seem to have particular targets, such as children or prostitutes. The most baffling of all are the cases where the killings are without motive. These murders are opportunistic and completely indiscriminate.

Harry Holmes designed his 'castle' for murdering, torturing and disposing of his victims.

Holmes, Dr Harry Howard (1890-95)

New Hampshire-born bigamist Harry Holmes, also known as Herman Webster Mudgett, acquired the nickname 'The Torture Doctor' due to his sinister activities. In 1890, Holmes' drugstore boss, Mrs Holden, disappeared and he subsequently inherited the business. This thrived sufficiently for him to build a 100-room hotel opposite the shop, and it was here that he developed his death house.

The Torture Doctor

When an insurance fraud led the police to search Holmes' hotel, they found a basement containing vats of acid, windowless torture rooms and a number of female bones and skeletons. He was brought to trial in 1895, where he represented himself. Found guilty of murder, he was hanged in May 1896. Before his death, he confessed his crimes to a newspaper, for which he was paid $7,500 – he had apparently committed a total of 27 murders.

See Harold Shipman p. 89

Komaroff, Vasili (1921-23)

Komaroff seemed to be the most unlikely killer: he was a contented family man and a Moscow horse trader. Only his closest friends knew he had once tried to kill his own son.

The Wolf of Moscow

Between 1921 and 1923, some 33 male bodies were found in sacks close to the Moscow horse market. Police made systematic searches of the area and, when they visited Komaroff's home, found his latest victim in the trademark sack. Robbery was the probable motive and all the victims had either been killed with a hammer or strangled. The 'Wolf of Moscow' had finally been discovered; he showed the police the resting place of his last five victims, though most of the bodies had been thrown into the river and were never recovered. Komaroff and his wife – who was implicated in the crimes – were shot by firing squad on 18 June 1923.

Petiot, Dr Marcel (1944)

Dr Marcel Petiot had attracted the attention of the police before World War II for drug trafficking activities, but was still a practising physician in Paris during the war. He posed as a member of the Resistance and offered help to Jews wishing to escape from occupied Europe. Once he had them in his power, he gave them lethal injections and stole their money and treasured possessions.

Human Remains

When he was arrested, the remains of 27 people were found, part-burned or ready for incineration. Petiot claimed they were German collaborators, admitting to having killed at least 63 individuals. He was found guilty of murder and executed on 26 May 1946.

See Harold Shipman p. 89

Greenwood, Vaughn Orrin (1964-75)

Vaughn Greenwood became known as the 'Skid Row Slasher', preying on vagrants in the Los Angeles area. He began his murderous career in 1964, but the 11 killings, which included nine slasher murders, were not connected until 1975. In a bizarre ritual, Greenwood cut his victims' throats, then scattered salt around the body, removed the shoes and placed them pointing towards the victim's feet.

The Slasher Arrested

Greenwood had been arrested on 3 February 1975 in connection with the attempted murder of two men in Hollywood. The following month, police linked him to the slasher murders, and formally charged him in January 1976. In January 1977, Greenwood was found guilty of nine murders and sentenced to life imprisonment. He was charged separately for the two early murders in 1964, but these were declared to have been a mistrial.

See Dennis Nilson p. 66

Manson, Charles (1969)

Charles Manson was an ex-convict and a dropout, but he had a magnetic personality that apparently made him irresistible to women. He assembled around him 'the family', a group of disciples who began occupation of a disused ranch in California in the summer of 1969. Manson was something of an early survivalist, believing that the end of civilization was nigh and that he and his 'family' would inherit the earth.

Manson Family Murders

Their first murder took place on 25 July 1969, when they killed Gary Hinman in an attempt to seize his inheritance. On 9 August the same year, they broke into the home of film director Roman Polanski and his wife, Sharon Tate. In an orgy of violence, the family slaughtered five people in this Beverley Hills massacre. But they were not content with this. Two days later, they murdered the LaBianca family.

The Trial

One of Manson's followers, Susan Atkins, was imprisoned for prostitution shortly afterwards and, through a confession to a fellow inmate, the authorities learned of the family's involvement in the two slaughters. They were rounded up in December 1969 and, after an extraordinary trial, most of the members of the family were sentenced to death, later reduced to life imprisonment. Manson will never be released.

See Anatoly Onoprienko p. 63

West, Fred and Rosemary (1970s-90s)

On 13 December 1994, Fred West was charged with 12 murders; his wife, Rosemary, would later be found guilty of 10 murders and sentenced to 10 life sentences. The Wests lived at 25 Cromwell Street, Gloucester, which had literally, over a period of many years, become a house of horrors. Fred's murderous tendencies pre-dated even meeting Rosemary.

The Cromwell Street Killings

The Wests lived a bizarre life of extreme sex, prostitution, rape, imprisonment and murder. Their cellar was a torture chamber, where Rose would entertain clients and Fred would murder women. A succession of young women and unfortunate family members were raped, strangled, suffocated and then buried within the grounds of the house; several unwanted children were also dispatched.

Police Investigation

It was only the tenacity of Detective Constable Hazel Savage, who was investigating the rape of a young girl, that linked the Wests with a series of disappearances. When the police finally searched the house, on 24 February 1994, no fewer than nine different sets of bones were found in the cellar alone. The forensic evidence was overwhelming and, rather than face trial, Fred West committed suicide at Winston Green Prison, Birmingham, on New Year's Day 1995.

See Delina Gonzales and Maria de Jesus p. 80

The Cromwell Street killers, Fred and Rosemary West.

Gaskins, Donald (1975)

The disappearance of a 13-year-old girl in South Carolina in 1975 took police on a sickening journey into the world of mass murderer Donald Gaskins. While investigating the disappearance, police found two graveyards, one containing six corpses, the other two. With the assistance of one-time associate, Walter Neely, the police identified Gaskins as the contract killer in all cases. Known as 'Pee Wee', Gaskins had strong connections with the underworld.

Gaskins Reveals the Truth

Under the influence of a truth serum, Gaskins admitted to 13 killings and was sentenced to eight life terms. Unrepentant, Gaskins accepted another contract while in prison, this time to kill Rudolph Tyner. He rigged up an intercom packed with dynamite and blew off the side of Tyner's head. For this, Gaskins was finally sent to the electric chair.

See Electrocution p. 249

Gray, Marvin (1975)

Marvin Gray described himself as 'a natural-born murderer' and said 'all I think about is killing people'. On 5 June 2001, Gray was convicted of the 1975 shooting of a bank worker in Denver, Colorado. During the trial, he was forced to represent himself, having made threats to his own legal counsel. He was repeatedly removed from the court and was restrained with leg irons on his wrists.

Polygraph Proof

Police had used polygraphs to confirm Gray's assertions that he had committed over 40 murders; the lie detectors confirmed at least 20 of the statements. Gray was subsequently given three life sentences, but police are still piecing together his evidence and trying to link him with other cases. Authorities believe he may kill again in prison in order to achieve his desire to be executed.

See Lie Detectors and Polygraphs p. 245

Shipman, Harold (1978-98)

Doctor Harold Shipman was Britain's most prolific serial killer. Opinions differ as to how many of his patients the deadly doctor dispatched with drug overdoses, but it may have been in excess of 300.

Ongoing Enquiries

To some extent, the enquiries are still ongoing and Shipman has been officially linked with the murders of 215 of his patients who died in his care between 1978 and 1998. However,

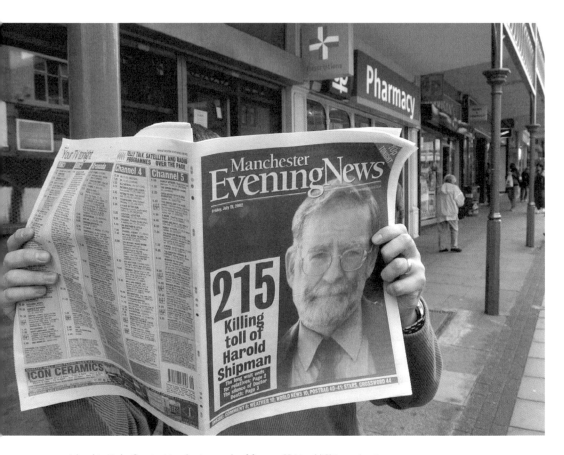

A local in Hyde, Greater Manchester, reads of former GP Harold Shipman's crimes.

there are several other cases of premature death, which may never be positively identified as Shipman killings. The huge disparity of deaths of his patients compared to those of other doctors in similar circumstances first began to sound alarm bells to his colleagues and later to the police. The enquiries were not well conducted and the police missed early opportunities to bring Shipman's crimes to light, thus allowing him to continue to murder. Shipman had made amateur attempts to cover his tracks by doctoring medical records and lying about the medical condition of many of his patients.

Trial and Death

His trial began in October 1999, and in January 2000, he was found guilty of 15 specimen murder charges and sentenced to life imprisonment for each conviction. He hanged himself in his prison cell in 2004.

Ramirez, Richard (1985)

Throughout 1985, Richard Ramirez terrorized Los Angeles and became known as the 'Night Stalker'. Ramirez would enter a home and shoot the male member of the family, then move on to rape and either beat or shoot the female and any children. Ramirez had a previous criminal record for theft and burglary, and when his stolen car number plate was given to the police by a witness, his fingerprints were found in the abandoned vehicle. After a large police hunt, he was recognized while attempting to steal a car. He confessed to the crimes but pleaded not guilty at his trial. Nonetheless, he was found guilty of 13 murders, plus other crimes, and Ramirez remains on death row.

Richard Ramirez displays a pentacle in a Los Angeles courtroom.

See Ted Bundy p. 71

male killers

Wife Killers

It is widely known that, in a high percentage of murder cases, the victim knows their killer. Often they are related – and the most common relationship in these cases is man and wife. Motivated by jealousy, rage, lust or even boredom, investigating officers usually turn first to the husband of a murdered woman.

Following an appeal 12 years on, Sam Sheppard is cleared of murder and leads his second wife from court.

Sheppard, Sam (1954)

In 1954, neurosurgeon Sam Sheppard claimed that his wife had been killed by an intruder to their home in Cleveland, Ohio. He also claimed to have been knocked unconscious twice by the same intruder. Circumstantial evidence led to the conviction of the doctor, despite his pleas of innocence. Twelve years later, in 1966, an appeal was lodged and Sheppard walked free. The 'bushy-haired intruder' has never been traced, although many still believe Sheppard murdered his own wife.

See Michael Fletcher p. 98

List, John (1971)

Following a television reconstruction in 1989, respectable accountant John Hardy was positively identified as John List, who had disappeared 17 years earlier, in 1971, after the entire List family – mother Alma, wife Helen, daughter Patricia and sons John Jr and Frederick – had all been slaughtered in their large Victorian home in New Jersey. List's car had been discovered at the airport, but he could not be traced.

Mercy Killing?

List, a strict Lutheran, claimed that he had killed his family to save them from a godless world. The police had retained fingerprint evidence, ballistics and autopsy reports, all of which damned List. He claimed that he could not kill himself because he would be sent to hell. He was found guilty of all five murders on 12 April 1990 and given five life sentences.

See Autopsies p. 124; Fingerprints p. 235

Davis, T. Cullen (1976)

T. Cullen Davis was one of the richest men in the United States, and the inspiration for the *Dallas* character, J. R. Ewing.

Cullen Denies the Charge

In August 1976, at the home of Davis's estranged wife in Mockingbird Lane, Fort Worth,

Texas, a black-clad assassin shot and killed Andrea Wilborn and Stan Farr, and grievously wounded Priscilla Davis, the supposed intended target, as well as Gus Gavrel, Jr. Priscilla positively identified her estranged husband, T. Cullen Davis, as the murderer. Cullen was charged but he had access to the best legal representation money could buy and claimed to have been in bed with his girlfriend at the time.

Acquittal

The defence suggested that Farr had been the real target with Priscilla behind the intended assassination. Cullen was ultimately acquitted, but in August 1978, an FBI informant, David McCrory, came forward to say that Cullen had given him a list of a dozen people to kill. The FBI faked a photograph of one of the targets, Judge Eidson, who was handling the Davis divorce and taped an incriminating conversation between Cullen and McCrory. Despite this, Cullen was again acquitted. Legal costs had crippled Davis and the murders remain unsolved.

Durst, Robert (1982–2002)

Despite having over $500 in his pocket, millionaire Robert Durst chose to steal a sandwich and a newspaper from a supermarket in Pennsylvania. He was caught and handed over to the police, who discovered to their amazement that the heavily disguised man was wanted for murders in Texas, Los Angeles and New York.

Durst's Victims

Durst's wife, Kathleen, had disappeared in New York in January 1982. On Christmas Eve 2000, Susan Berman – a long-time friend of Durst – was found shot in her home in Los Angeles. This was believed to have been a contract killing. In September 2001, a human torso was discovered in Galveston, Texas. The body was later identified as Morris Black. Durst was picked up nine days later and linked to the murder, but was given a $300,000 bail and promptly disappeared, until he was picked up once more in Pennsylvania. Durst was sent back to Texas in January 2002; he would claim that he killed Black in self defence. Legal arguments continue, with all three US states eager to convict Durst of the three killings,

despite the lack of conclusive evidence to place him at the scenes of the murders. He
received parole in 2005.

See T. Cullen Davis p. 95

Douglas, Scott Stuart (1991)

The marriage of Scott Stuart and Ann Scripps had broken down by 1991. Ann, a rich heiress,
had married the younger Scott, who favoured the high life. Whilst she was petitioning a
court in New York to have Scott removed from the house, he bludgeoned Ann to death,
leaving his car at a bridge. The family believed he had faked suicide, but in 1994, his body
was found on the banks of the Hudson River.

See Michael Fletcher p. 98

Gingerich, Edward (1993)

Edward Gingerich murdered his wife Katie in Crawford County, Pennsylvania, in 1993. He has
the distinction of being the only Amish man to have been convicted of murder. He killed and

An Amish farmer in Pennsylvania. Edward Gingerich remains the only Amish man to have been
convicted of murder.

disembowelled his wife in a schizophrenic frenzy that was witnessed by his two children. He was found guilty of involuntary manslaughter. At the time, he had stopped taking medication for paranoid schizophrenia for nine months. Gingerich was released from prison in March 1998.

See John List p. 95

Abequa, Mohammed (1994)

Jordanian-born Mohammed Abequa married Nina Gussal in January 1986. The couple lived in New Jersey and had two children, Sami and Lisa. The previously happy marriage fell apart in 1989 and they began a custody battle for their children. In July 1994, Abequa strangled his wife, then fled to Jordan with the children. It took the intercession of King Hussein of Jordan to secure the return of the children to their family in America.

Trial in Jordan

In 1994, Abequa was tried in a Jordanian court and sentenced to 15 years imprisonment; he was released in 2000. Nina's US-based family still live in constant fear that Abequa will return to retrieve his children. The children live with their mother's sister, Nesime Dokur.

Fletcher, Michael (1999)

In 1999, the pregnant Leann Fletcher was shot and killed in Macon County, Michigan. Her husband Michael had called the police from the crime scene, claiming that she had committed suicide. Investigators were suspicious, however, and Fletcher soon became the prime suspect.

The Jury's Findings

It took jurors only 15 minutes to rule out the possibility of suicide or accidental shooting. They took four days to agree that it had been a premeditated murder, based on the fact that the couple had separated on several occasions and were known to be at loggerheads. The judge found Fletcher guilty of the murder of Leann and her unborn child. He will remain in prison until at least 2017.

Child Killers

Opportunistic male killers usually attack lone females. Children are harder to take, as they are usually accompanied. However, this has not prevented some of the most notorious murder cases being those of children.

Griffiths, Peter (1948)

The abduction of three-year-old June Anne Devaney from Queen's Park Hospital, Blackburn, and her subsequent murder, saw the first mass fingerprinting exercise in the UK. The young girl was snatched from a children's ward in the early hours of 15 May 1948. Her body was found before dawn; she had been molested and had died from terrible head injuries.

Fingerprint Evidence

The police found 642 sets of fingerprints on the ward, tracing and eliminating all those who had a legitimate reason to enter the hospital over the past two years. One set of prints was left unaccounted for. Between June and July, the police collected in excess of 50,000 prints, cross-referencing the electoral register and rationing cards. In this way, they followed a trail to Peter Griffiths who, damned by the evidence, was hanged on 19 November 1948.

See Fingerprints p. 235

Nelson, Dale (1970)

Dale Nelson went on a killing spree in September 1970, after a serious drinking binge created in him an uncontrollable rage. He first visited his distant relative Shirley Wasyk's house in British Columbia, Canada, killing her and one of her children and raping another. Nelson then drove to the Phipps' family home, killing Ray and Isabelle and three of their four children, then abducted their eight-year-old daughter Cathy; the following day, her body was found horribly mutilated.

Consequences of the Killing Spree

Nelson was caught sleeping off the effects of the alcohol. He was found guilty of all eight murders and was sentenced to life imprisonment in April 1971. The sheer violence, particularly in the Wasyks' house, shocked the Canadian community near the US border. It was said that after killing Tracy Wasyk, Nelson cut her stomach open and ate the contents.

The Sarah Payne Case (2000)

On 1 July 2000, eight-year-old Sarah Payne went missing in Kingston Gorse, Sussex. A local man on the sex offenders register soon became the prime suspect. Over 500 items were submitted for forensic analysis; more than 20 experts in the fields of entomology, pathology, geology, archaeology and environmental profiling were deployed after Sarah's body was found on 17 July.

Forensics Point the Way

The first breakthrough was a link between Sarah's shoe and the suspect's sweatshirt; then fibres from his van were found in her hair and her DNA was found on his clothing. The police had seized the suspect's van, where they found the sweatshirt, a pair of socks, a shirt, a pair of

curtains and a petrol receipt that placed the suspect near where Sarah's body had been found. Sarah's shoe had trapped 350 fibres on the Velcro fastener and some of these matched the sweatshirt. On the sweatshirt, one of the 40 hairs matched Sarah's DNA profile. A single multi-coloured cotton fibre on the shoe was found to match the curtains.

Roy Whiting

In December 2001, Roy Whiting was found guilty and sentenced to life imprisonment, despite objections to some of the forensic evidence. The trial judge, Richard Curtis, recommended that the life term should mean life.

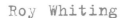

See Fibre Analysis p. 241

Eight-year-old Sarah Payne, who was murdered in 2000.

Sexual Predators

Male killers are often motivated by sexual desires or fantasies. Their victims are often subjected to rape before they are killed, sometimes in a ritualistic way. Often, these men are opportunistic, attacking women who are out alone.

Hoch, Johann (1895–1906)

German-born Johann Schmidt adopted the name Hoch around 1895, the name being the maiden name of his first wife and his first victim. Hoch travelled around the United States, meeting women through lonely hearts advertisements, after which he bigamously married them. He is believed to have murdered at least 15 of them.

Arsenic Poisoning

Hoch's chosen method of murder was arsenic poisoning; the poison was found in his fountain pen when he was finally arrested. He was hanged on 23 February 1906. In 1955, a pile of bones found hidden in the walls of a Chicago house were linked to Hoch. It is believed that he married at least 55 women and that such was his desire to obtain money from them that, on one occasion, he even removed gold false teeth from a glass of water beside his wife's bed.

See Henri Desire Landru p. 109

Heirens, William (1945–46)

William Heirens was a Chicago-based burglar and arsonist who turned to murder in 1945. For him, crime was an outlet for his suppressed sexuality; he claimed to feel physically sick when he touched a woman. This aversion did not prevent him from mutilating and killing Josephine Ross, Frances Brown and six-year-old Suzanne Degnan. The first murder probably took place as a result of being discovered whilst burgling Ross's apartment.

The 17-year-old William Heirens, who was sentenced to 71 years imprisonment in 1946.

Handwriting Analysis

When he was arrested in 1946, handwriting tests linked him with a note left at the scene of the Brown murder, which read 'for heaven's sake catch me before I kill more. I cannot control myself.' Heirens claimed he was controlled by a malignant alter-ego he called George Murman, but this did not prevent him from being sentenced to three life terms in prison.

See Forensic Handwriting p. 243

Lashley, David (1970-89)

Jamie Shepherd disappeared on the night of 4 February 1977; her grave in Hertfordshire was not discovered until 18 April. She had been bound, raped and strangled.

Police Find a Suspect

During the investigation, police became suspicious of David Lashley, who had raped five women in 1970 and had also been convicted of a vicious attack, in which the victim miraculously survived, in July 1976. Lashley was charged with this attack and sentenced to 15 years. He was released on 7 February 1989 but was re-arrested after just 30 seconds and charged with the Shepherd murder. New DNA evidence from 13-year-old semen samples and testimony from inmates to whom Lashley had confided in prison proved damning, and he was sentenced to life imprisonment. After 13 years, DNA profiling had positively linked Lashley to the scene.

See DNA Testing p. 238

Jackson, Calvin (1973-74)

In 1973, Calvin Jackson began a series of burglaries and murders in New York, primarily targeting older, solitary women in a poorer part of the city. Jackson worked at the Park Plaza Hotel, which became the epicentre of the murders. He killed Theresa Jordan in April 1973 and murdered Kate Lewisohn shortly after this. In April the following year, he murdered Mabel Hartmeyer and Yeria Vishnefsky. In June 1974, he killed Winifred Miller and Blanche Vincent; in July, Martha Carpenter, and finally, in August, Eleanor Platt and Pauline Spanierman. All the victims had been strangled, and raped both before and after death. Jackson was linked to the murders when Spanierman's television was found in his room. He confessed to the killings and was sentenced to 18 consecutive life terms.

See John Glover p. 106

Bittaker, Lawrence and Norris, Roy (1979)

Lawrence Bittaker and Roy Norris met in prison. After their release, they planned a series of rapes and murders in the Los Angeles area.

Roy Norris (right) is charged with murder, rape and burglary.

Victims

Cindy Schaeffer's body was found in June 1979 and in July, they abducted, raped and murdered Andrea Joy Hall. This was followed in September by the murders of Jackie Gilliam and Leah Lamp. Shirley Ledford fell victim on Halloween. Between the double murder and the Halloween killing, Bittaker and Norris had raped another woman but had released her – a fatal mistake, as she was able to give the police enough information to catch the two men.

Confession

Norris confessed to the murders and showed the police where the bodies had been hidden. He claimed Bittaker had taken the leading role but both were charged with five rapes, robberies, kidnappings and murders. Norris testified against Bittaker to avoid the death sentence and was given 45 years. Bittaker remains on death row.

Duffy, John Francis and Mulcahy, David (1982-86)

Between 1982 and 1986, railway carpenter John Duffy committed at least 26 rapes in the London area. Duffy attempted to remove all evidence by scrupulously cleaning the women after the attacks. Rape turned to murder with the killings of Anne Lock, Alison Day and Maartje Tamboezer.

Further Murders

Ultimately, Duffy would be convicted of the Day and Tamboezer murders and of five rapes. He was positively linked to the Tamboezer murder when traces of his semen were found on her

John Duffy (left) and David Mulcahy

body and fibres of his clothing were discovered on Day's jacket. Lock's body was so decomposed that there was insufficient scientific evidence to link Duffy with her murder. Another damning piece of evidence was the British Rail string used to tie the victims. On 26 February 1988, he was sentenced to 30 years. Ten years into this sentence, he implicated his childhood friend, David Mulcahy, as his accomplice. Mulcahy was sentenced to life imprisonment in 1999.

See DNA Testing p. 238

Dupas, Peter (1983-99)

Between 1974 and 1994, Australian Peter Dupas was convicted several times for sexual offences, including rape, and his offences were becoming increasingly violent. In March 1999, he murdered Nicole Patterson in Melbourne, stabbing her 30 times.

Solving the Unsolved Crimes

Dupas was caught and given life imprisonment; from this time, he became the focus of several unsolved murders in the Melbourne area. It is believed that his first victim was Helen McMahon, who was raped and killed in February 1983 at the exact location where Dupas had raped another woman a few weeks before. He was also linked with the murder of Mersina Halvagis, who was stabbed to death in a Melbourne cemetery. In February 2002, DNA evidence linked Dupas with the murder of Margaret Maher, who had been stabbed and killed in October 1997.

See DNA Testing p. 238

Code, Nathaniel Jr (1984-87)

Nathaniel Code Jr was released from prison in 1984 after serving two years for rape. He married, and seemed a reformed man. This was not the case, however. On 31 August 1984, he murdered Debra Ford, and the following year, he slaughtered a whole family just a short distance from his home in Shreveport, Louisiana.

The Final Murder

On 5 August 1987, he killed his own grandfather, William, and the two young grandsons of a friend. Code was known to hate his grandfather and was questioned by police in the wake of the killing; fingerprints from the scene matched the other family slaughter in 1985 and he was charged, tried and convicted of multiple murders. Code is still in the process of appealing against the death sentence, but will never be freed, so violent and atrocious were his crimes.

See George Banks p.48

Gary Heidnik, the psychotic sex killer who kidnapped women and took them to his 'cellar of death'.

Heidnik, Gary (1986)

In 1978, Gary Heidnik was jailed for four years for kidnap and rape. After his release, he began to assemble a harem of sex slaves by kidnapping women in the New Jersey area. By 1986, some five women were imprisoned in Heidnik's basement, where they were tortured and raped, and where two were eventually murdered. One of the women managed to escape and Heidnik was convicted and sentenced to death, a sentence carried out by lethal injection on 6 July 1999.

See Lethal Injection p. 251

Glover, John Wayne (1989-91)

John Wayne Glover was nicknamed 'The Granny Killer' – his victims were six elderly women in Sydney, Australia, and Glover murdered them all in just over a year. He claimed his first victim in March 1989, forcing Gwendolin Mitchelhill into a side street, where he hit her on the head with a hammer, raped her and then strangled her. This was the same technique he would use on the next four women whose lives he claimed. He also carried out a series of rapes at nursing homes in the Sydney area. It was only when he murdered Joan Sinclair, a woman known to him, that he was finally arrested and charged with a total of six murders. He stood trial in November 1991 and was sentenced to life imprisonment.

See Calvin Jackson p. 103

Evonitz, Richard (1996-2002)

It took forensic examinations of fibres found in Richard Evonitz's apartment to positively link him with at least three abductions, rapes and murders in Virginia.

Murder Methods

Sofia Silva disappeared on 9 September 1996 whilst doing homework on her own front doorstep. Her body was discovered six weeks later. On 1 May 1997, sisters Kristin and Kati Lisk disappeared after getting off their school bus in Fredericksburg. The two were found dead five days later. All three victims had been strangled or suffocated and then dumped in water.

Suicide Before Capture

Evonitz made his fatal mistake in June 2002 in South Carolina. He had abducted a girl, raped her and then fallen asleep, allowing her to escape. Police finally caught up with him in Florida, but he killed himself before he could be arrested.

See Fibre Analysis p. 241

Kee, Arohn (2000)

In December 2000, Arohn Kee was found guilty of 22 crimes, including murder, rape and robbery, and was sentenced to life imprisonment in January 2001. He had murdered three young girls in the Harlem area: Johalis Castro, Rasheda Taylor and Paola Illera. It was also established that he had raped at least another four women. Kee had been under surveillance and when he was arrested on a theft charge, a DNA sample was taken from a cup he had used whilst being questioned. This linked him to the rapes and murders. Kee fled to Miami, Florida, but was picked up in the company of a 17-year-old girl who police believed would have been his next victim. Kee was sentenced to a total of 400 years for his crimes.

See DNA Testing p. 238

DNA samples are loaded into a DNA sequencer. A DNA sample taken from a cup used by Arohn Kee while he was being questioned over a theft charge linked him to many rapes and murders.

Money-Motivated Murders

Money is a powerful motive for murder. Some criminals may start out as swindlers and conmen, but their greed can drive them to murder. Others will carry out calculated killings if they think it will win them financial rewards.

Deeming, Frederick Bailey (1891-92)

Liverpool-born Frederick Bailey Deeming was a bigamist, swindler, thief and murderer, using aliases to perpetrate a number of crimes in Australia, England and South Africa.

The Deceptive Baron

In 1891, using the name Williams, he posed as an agent for a baron in the Liverpool area, obtaining a rent-free villa. Although married with four children, he began courting Emily Mather, the villa-owner's daughter. He murdered and buried his wife Maria and all their children, and married Emily. The newlyweds arrived in Melbourne, Australia, in December 1891; by the end of the first month, Emily had also been killed. The Australian police caught Deeming in March 1892, by which time he was posing as Baron Swanton and had become engaged to Katie Rounsefell. Deeming was hanged for his crimes on 23 May 1892.

See Hanging p. 247

Landru, Henri Désiré (1915-19)

In a five-year killing spree, Frenchman Henri Désiré Landru murdered 11 women – although there were allegations that the figure may have

France's infamous war widow killer, Henri Désiré Landru.

been as high as 300. The First World War had left many women widows; Landru plundered their assets, either using confidence tricks to control their life savings or acquiring them on the deaths of the women. He disposed of the majority of the bodies in the kitchen stove. Landru was executed by guillotine on 25 February 1922.

See Johann Hoch p. 101

Mills loses gamble for life

JURY FINDS HIM GUILTY OF ORCHARD MURDER

Express Staff Reporter: Nottingham, Thursday

AT 19, Herbert Leonard Mills was sentenced to death today. He said he was a gambler; he said he was a liar. And a jury of 11 men and one woman decided he was a murderer.

He gambled with his life as calmly as—when he was only 15—he gambled hundreds of pounds in cash. He lost as calmly. He stood, arms folded, beneath a cluster of electric lamps at Nottingham Assizes and heard the sentence. When he was asked if he had anything to say, he replied firmly: "No, nothing."

His father, a miner, was sitting in court. Mills ignored him. He jerked his head and looked up to the crowded public gallery; and then he turned away.

Mills's counsel, Mr. Richard Elwes, K.C., had told the jury: "If you are ever going to see a man who has gambled with his life and is composed"—Mr. Elwes dropped his voice to a whisper—"whether he wins or loses, you are seeing one now."

"It is a most unusual murder trial. In one way it is almost unique . . . There is not one shred of sympathy for this man, and I should be the last to expect it."

'No sadist'

Mills was found guilty of strangling Mrs. Mabel Tattershaw, who was 30 years older than him, in a derelict orchard known as "The Jungle."

Mrs. Tattershaw—her husband is in prison—had two daughters. Mills, who was said to have an aversion to women, met her in a Nottingham cinema the day before she was killed.

In his defence, it was argued that this was a sadistic murder, and Mills was no sadist. Love of the limelight, the jury was told, landed him in the dock.

For Mills said he found the body, and decided to make money by phoning a newspaper before he told the police.

He wrote a confession. In court he said this was bogus, invented to get more money. Yes, he would tell anyone a lie if it was to his benefit. Yes, his desire for money was such that he would stop at nothing.

The prosecution analysed the confession. Twelve facts in it were proved true—and counsel claimed that the rest, dealing with the killing, was also true.

'He was bitter'

Hairs similar to Mills's were found on Mrs. Tattershaw. Fibres under her fingernails matched those in Mills's blue suit. And how odd, said coun-

Slimming judge tells man: Lose weight

JUDGE DALE, who has been having trouble with his waist-line, gave some advice yesterday to a man faced with a similar problem. The advice? Take a slimming course.

The man, a 16-stoner, was sued in Westminster County Court by a firm of Dover-street tailors for £44 8s. 6d., the balance of the price of three suits.

He counter-claimed for £66 5s. he had paid to the tailors. He said the suits did not fit, and never had fitted.

Two inches bigger

But the man was measured in court, and his chest, waist and hip measurements were at least two inches bigger than when he ordered the suits.

The man said he had been on the Continent. Then Judge Dale said:—

"I had a month in France a short while ago and, unfortunately, put on nearly six inches round the waist. I am getting it off now."

He gave judgment for the

NEW TURN IN
Mystery in MacEv

From THOMAS CLAYTON

SOME news came from Commissioner Lea wreck of the Kangaro look which Claude Ra throughout the film "

For the Cannes police confirmed that Freddie MacEvoy's yacht Kangaroa had a passenger aboard when she sailed from the Riviera on her last trip.

The passenger was an American.

The three survivors at first denied there had been a passenger. Confronted with police evidence today, however, survivor Willy Gehring admitted it.

A 'GRILLING'

He said the American left the yacht at Ibiza—which is the port

IN CELL NEXT TO DEAD WOMAN'S HUSBAND...

THE face of Herbert Leonard Mills. . . . When he was first arrested he was put in a cell in Lincoln jail. In the next cell was William

woman Mills has been found guilty of murdering. Trouble threatened. Whispers passed along the prison "grapevine" —and Tattershaw, serving two years for shopbreaking, was

The outcome of the Mills murder trial is reported in the *Daily Express* in November 1951.

Mills, Herbert Leonard (1951)

Herbert Leonard Mills met his victim at a Nottingham cinema on 2 August 1951. Mabel Tatters Law was a 48-year-old mother of two. The day after they met, Mabel – flattered by the attentions of the 19-year-old Mills – consented to go with him into a local woodland area. There he beat and strangled her to death.

The Perfect Murder?

The case then took a bizarre twist, as Mills called the *News of the World* and offered them an exclusive on the murder, claiming that he had just discovered the body. The police were informed and Mills was interviewed. During this period, Mills gave increasingly lurid descriptions of his 'discovery' to the press in return for money. The statements culminated in a confession to the *News of the World* on 14 August, after which he was charged with the murder and hanged in December of the same year. It seems his motive had simply been to commit the perfect murder.

See Arthur and Nazimodeen Hosein p. 112

Merrett, John Donald (1954)

New Zealander John Merrett moved to Edinburgh with his mother in 1925. After forging several cheques in her name, he murdered her, but set up the scene so it looked like an accidental shooting. He was cleared of the murder charge, serving only eight months for fraud.

Marriage and Murder

Adopting the name John Ronald Chesney, he married Vera Bonner in 1929, who had inherited £50,000. They separated in 1953 and Merrett moved to Germany. However, his wife had £8,400 in trust and this would become Merrett's on her death. On 10 February 1954, Merrett returned to the UK under an assumed name. He rendered his wife unconscious through drink and drowned her in a bath, then battered her mother to death. Fibre traces on his clothing confirmed his guilt, but Merrett chose suicide rather than facing the hangman; he died by his own hand in Germany six days later.

See Fibre Analysis p. 241

Hickock, Richard and Smith, Perry (1959)

The four members of the Clutter family who were found dead in their Kansas home in 1959.

On the night of 14 November 1959, Richard Hickock and Perry Smith broke into the home of the Clutter family in Holcomb, Kansas. Unable to find much of value, they stole $50, a radio and a pair of binoculars – and murdered Herbert Clutter, his wife Bonnie and their children Nancy and Kenyon. The killers set off for Mexico, where they tried to sell the stolen radio; the move turned out to be their downfall, as this helped police pick up their trail and they were arrested in Las Vegas in January 1960. They confessed to the burglary and murders. Hickock and Smith were sentenced to death on 29 March 1960, and the sentences were duly carried out by hanging on 14 April 1965.

See Ronald DeFeo p. 115

Hosein, Arthur and Nizamodeen (1970)

By all accounts, Trinidad-born Arthur Hosein was an accomplished tailor, yet he had chosen to live beyond his means when he bought Rooks Farm in Stocking Pelham, Hertfordshire. In a desperate attempt to raise money, he and his brother Nizamodeen planned to kidnap the wife of media millionaire Rupert Murdoch. Instead, they kidnapped Muriel McKay, the wife of the Deputy Chairman of the *News of the World*.

Kidnap

She was taken from her home on 29 December 1970. Undeterred by the error, the brothers made a series of telephone calls and sent notes and letters to the newspaper's editor, demanding a ransom of £1 million. They made bodged attempts to collect the ransom money and were possibly frightened off by a large undercover police presence at the pickup point. The brothers' car was spotted in the area and they were linked by fingerprints and handwriting to the ransom notes.

Life Imprisonment

Although the brothers were positively linked to the kidnapping, they never admitted killing McKay and her body was never found. It is strongly believed, however, that the body was fed to the pigs on Rooks Farm. The brothers were sentenced to life for murder and given concurrent sentences for kidnapping and blackmail.

See Forensic Handwriting p. 243

Nizamodeen Hosein who, along with his brother, kidnapped and murdered Muriel McKay.

Menendez, Lyle and Erik (1989)

On the night of 20 August 1989, Erik and Lyle Menendez claimed they had returned home to their parents' luxury house in Beverley Hills to discover that their father, José, had been shot eight times and their mother, Kitty, five times. Both were dead. José was a successful Cuban-American businessman and the boys claimed he had subjected them to years of child abuse.

Money Motive

When the brothers were charged with their parents' murder in March 1990, the motive seemed to be the enormous inheritance they would receive. Indeed, they had gone on a huge spending spree in the months after the death of their parents. In a complex and lengthy court case, with much contradictory evidence, the brothers were found guilty on 20 March 1996 and sentenced to two consecutive life prison sentences.

See Ronald DeFeo p. 115

Strange Cases

These are the cases that defy categorization – the ones that led police on wild goose chases and had them baffled – for a time, at least. In the end, though, they got their man...

Dominici, Gaston (1952)

On 5 August 1952, French police received a call from a man named Gustave Dominici. He said he had discovered the bodies of the British biochemist Sir Jack Drummond, his wife Ann and their 11-year-old daughter, Elizabeth. The family had been shot whilst on a camping holiday near Marseille.

Gaston Dominici, who was found guilty of killing Sir Jack Drummond and family in 1954.

The Police Hunt

Gustave and his brother Clouis worked for their father, Gaston, on the family's farm, Grand Terre, just 150 m (500 ft) from the murder scene. For some weeks, the police found no leads on the killer, although they had their suspicions about the Dominici family, and relentlessly pursued them, hoping one would crack. The brothers finally pointed the fingers at their father. Gaston admitted to having been discovered by Sir Jack watching his wife undress; in the ensuing struggle, he had shot the Englishman, then killed Ann and Elizabeth. At 75 years of age, Gaston was spared the guillotine and released from prison in 1960.

DeFeo, Ronald (1974)

On the evening of 13 November 1974, the Amityville Police Department received information from a bar owner that a young man had reported the shooting of his mother and father. The man, Ronald 'Butch' DeFeo Jr, claimed his father had found himself on the wrong side of the mafia and that, two weeks previously, they had been behind an armed robbery at his father's business. Inside the DeFeo home, High Hopes, the police found the bodies of wealthy car dealer Ronald Sr, his wife Louise, daughters Dawn and Allison, and young sons Mark and John.

Convicted Sociopath

The police found that the murder weapon was Butch's own rifle and his claim of mafia involvement could not be substantiated; he was charged and put on trial for the murders. Butch's defence

Ronald DeFeo, who killed his entire family in their Amityville home in New York.

claimed insanity and also stated that he killed his family before they could kill him. The court took the view that he was a sociopath and had slaughtered his family as he felt little for them. Butch was sentenced to six concurrent life sentences. The case would have been all but forgotten except for the experience of the family who bought High Hopes; after a year, they were driven out of their home by evil spirits, providing the inspiration for the Amityville Horror movies.

See Lyle and Erik Menendez p. 113

Gilmore, Gary (1976)

Gary Gilmore, who insisted that his death penalty be carried out immediately.

Gilmore was sentenced to death for the murder of a motel clerk in Provo, Utah, on 20 July 1976. He also faced charges – but was never brought to trial – for another killing in Crem, Utah, the previous day.

Gilmore's Death Wish

What is particularly significant about Gilmore is not the scope of his killings, but his desire to die; indeed, he fought the US legal system for years to gain the right to be executed. He was an incorrigible criminal who had spent 18 years of the last 20 of his life in prison. He had twice attempted suicide and on three occasions, his execution had been delayed at the last moment. The US Supreme Court had suspended the death penalty between 1972 and 1976 and Gilmore became the first convicted murderer to be executed after this period. He was shot by firing squad on 17 January 1977; his last words as a hood was placed over his head were, 'Let's do it'. Gilmore's body was donated to the Utah Medical Center for medical research.

See Firing Squad p. 250

Feltner, Jeffrey Lynn (1988)

In 1988, the police received a telephone call from a man claiming to have committed a series of murders at a nursing home in Melrose, Florida. Investigation showed there had been only one sudden death at the nursing home, on 10 February 1988. As a result, Jeffrey Feltner, who had made the call, received four months imprisonment for making false statements. Whilst incarcerated, he discovered he had developed AIDS. On his release, Feltner again began making nuisance calls to the police, but he was linked to the murder of a pensioner at Daytona Beach. He told police he was indeed guilty of the sudden death, as well as four other murders at the Melrose nursing home, plus another at a medical centre. In January 1989, Feltner was given a life sentence with no chance of parole for 25 years.

See Robert Diaz p. 48

Denyer, Paul Charles (1993)

A blow to the head as a child was the apparent reason that Paul Charles Denyer turned to murder later in life. As a child, he had cut a kitten's throat and had attacked school friends. He had trouble fitting in at school, due to his size, and was regarded as something of a loner. On leaving school, Denyer had numerous jobs, but did not hold them down for long due to his laziness and his aggressive behaviour; he was fired from his supermarket job after deliberately knocking over a woman and child with a line of empty shopping trolleys.

Fear On The Streets

In 1992 he moved in to a flat with his girlfriend, Sharon Johnson, in Frankstone, near Melbourne. In 1993 he became known as the Frankston Serial Killer, claiming the lives of three women – chosen at random – all of whom were slashed and stabbed to death. His blood had been found on one of the victims, and with such overwhelming evidence Denyer confessed to the murders. He said that he had been stalking women in Frankston for many years, admitting to a hatred a women in general, and confessing 'I've always wanted to kill, waiting for the right time, waiting for that silent alarm to trigger me off'. In December 1993, before a Melbourne court, he pleaded guilty and was sentenced to 30 years with no possibility of parole.

See Serology p. 239

5

Man-Haters

Some women just don't like men. For the women in this section, that dislike turned to hatred – and hatred turned to murder. These female predators deliberately selected male victims to vent their murderous feelings.

Ford, Clara (1894)

Clara Ford desperately hated male attention and so she often wore men's clothes in an effort to avoid it. In 1894, when Benjamin Westwood made improper advances towards her, she shot him. Life for this mixed-race woman in turn-of-the-century Toronto had been difficult and despite her colour, the jury was impressed with her independence and indignation. She was cleared of the charge and it transpired that Westwood had previously seduced Clara's daughter.

Wuornos, Aileen (1989-90)

Between November 1989 and June 1990, the roadside prostitute Aileen 'Lee' Wuornos claimed the lives of seven of her clients, usually white middle-aged men. Wuornos showed the hallmarks of a serial killer: abandoned by a teenage mother, ill-treated by an alcoholic grandfather, an early pregnancy herself, drink, drugs and a move into prostitution to support her habits.

Death penalty protesters pictured before the execution of Aileen Wuornos.

Prostitution and Despair

Wuornos drifted around the US until 1976; she would later claim that she had been raped and beaten by clients on at least 12 occasions. Finally, she settled at Daytona Beach, Florida. Unable to establish long-term relationships with men, she attempted to commit suicide on several occasions.

Killing Clients

By 1986, she had formed a tempestuous lesbian relationship with Tyria Moore, although she still earned her living as a highway prostitute. Wuornos was tired of being brutalized and ripped off by her clients and now packed a pistol. She killed first in November 1989, then six more times before Moore was picked up and turned against her. In January and May 1992, Wuornos was found guilty of four of the seven killings connected with her, and she was sentenced to death.

Smart, Pamela (1990)

In 1991 Pamela Smart was sentenced to life imprisonment for plotting the murder of her husband, Gregory. The New Hampshire trial, which was the first fully-televised case in the US and watched by millions across the country, featured the 22-year-old Pamela and her 15-year-old lover William Flynn, whom she had met at the school where she worked. Their relationship had started after they discovered a mutual love of heavy-metal music. Pamela was unhappy in her marriage to Gregory, and it was alleged that she persuaded 'Billy' and three accomplices to fake a break-in and murder her husband.

The Ice Princess

The police soon linked Flynn with Pamela, and he and two of the accomplices testified against her. The press nicknamed her the 'Ice Princess'. She was found guilty and sentenced to life with no opportunity of parole. The four young men were all sentenced to long prison terms for their involvement in the killing.

See Betty Broderick p. 140

Old People Killers

There are several well-known cases where the elderly have been targeted by female killers. Often preyed on by people in a position of control over them, these vulnerable members of society have fallen victim to some of the cruellest of crimes.

Webster, Kate (1879)

Irish-born Kate Webster already had a criminal record for robbery when she committed murder in 1879. It is known that at some point she had been living with a man, by whom she had a son; by 1877, they had both abandoned her, and perhaps it was this that drove her to kill.

From Maid to Murderer

In January 1879, Kate moved to Richmond to take a position as maid to a wealthy retired schoolteacher named Julia Thomas. Less than two months later, she ambushed the old lady at the top of the stairs, hit her and threw her down the stairs, then strangled her. She dragged the body into the kitchen, laid it on the table, removed the head with a meat saw and dismembered the body with a carving knife. She heated up a large copper pan of water to boil the body parts, then began selling Mrs Thomas's body fat as 'best dripping' to her neighbours.

Flight and Arrest

Mrs Thomas's disappearance soon aroused suspicion, however, and Kate fled to Ireland; she was arrested there shortly afterwards. She denied any knowledge of the murder, but was found guilty and sentenced to death. She was hanged in Wandsworth Prison on 29 July 1879.

See Hanging p. 247

Hahn, Anna (1937)

German-born Anna Hahn preyed on elderly men in the Cincinnati area in the 1930s, poisoning them with a mixture of croton oil and arsenic. She posed as an official nurse and seduced men to secure their inheritances before dispatching them. She claimed two victims in one week in June 1937, prompting the police to exhume the bodies. The 'angel of mercy', as she called herself, was undone and was electrocuted on 7 December 1938.

See Electrocution p. 249

Poison is the most popular murder method among women and was used by killers such as Anna Hahn.

Graham, Gwendolyn and Wood, Catherine (1988)

Lesbian nurses Gwendolyn Graham and Catherine Wood worked together at the Alpine Manor Nursing Home in Michigan. They took to murdering elderly women in their care and making love whilst they washed the bodies. Six victims were claimed until Graham found a new lover and Wood told her ex-husband of the killings.

Trial and Conviction

The police, using Wood as their star witness, succeeded in convicting Graham of six counts of murder, earning her life imprisonment without prospect of parole. Wood attempted to put the bulk of the blame on her ex-lover; despite explaining to the court that Graham had suffocated the victims and that she had taken a minor role in the killings. She received a minimum of 20 years at the conclusion of the trial in 1988.

Child Killers

Some of the most shocking examples of female killers are the cases in which women murder children. Sometimes, these have been young people in their care, or even their own children. In other cases, they are unknown to the killer, who has just attacked them, seemingly without motive.

Brownrigg, Elizabeth (1767)

Elizabeth Brownrigg was undoubtedly one of the most sadistic psychopaths of the eighteenth century. She and her husband had 16 children of their own and took in many of the poor and disadvantaged women and children in their neighbourhood in Greenwich, London. Over several years, she systematically tortured and imprisoned a number of girls and women charged to her care and is believed to have murdered at least 13 of her own children.

Brownrigg's Apprentices

The authorities investigated Brownrigg in 1767 after numerous accusations of cruelty to her 'apprentices'. The Brownriggs fled but were arrested in Wandsworth and subsequently tried at the Old Bailey. Elizabeth Brownrigg was found guilty of murder and sentenced to death, but her husband James and son John were acquitted and given just six months imprisonment for acts of cruelty.

Elizabeth Brownrigg, who treated her apprentices with terrible cruelty.

Eleventh-Hour Confession

On 14 September 1767, before being taken to Tyburn to be executed, Elizabeth confessed her crimes to a clergyman. There were enormous crowds lining the streets and the hangman immediately carried out the sentence for fear that she would be lynched before he could accomplish his task. After the execution, her body was dissected and her skeleton was hung in the Surgeon's Hall.

See Amelia Dyer p. 126

Kent, Constance (1860)

Constance Kent may have been the victim of a miscarriage of justice that cost her 20 years imprisonment, for despite the fact that she pleaded guilty to the murder of her three-year-old half-brother, Francis, the evidence suggests that she was not the perpetrator of the crime.

Murder at Road Hill House

Constance's father had remarried shortly after the death of his first wife and the new Mrs Kent – Miss Pratt, a former governess – soon gave birth to a son. Young Francis disappeared from the family home near Trowbridge, Wiltshire, on 30 June 1860 and his body was later discovered in an outside privy; his throat had been cut so deeply that his head was nearly severed. Suspicion fell on Constance, who had been badly treated by her stepmother and was known to have resented Francis's arrival. The evidence was circumstantial, though, and Constance was never charged.

Miscarriage of Justice?

Surprisingly, however, on 25 April 1864, she confessed to the crime. Her description of how she had killed the boy contradicted police observations: she claimed to have cut his throat with a razor, but the child had been suffocated and then the wound inflicted. It seems possible that the murder was carried out by her father, with the help of the governess and nurse, Elizabeth Gough, although no motive could be established. Constance was released from prison in 1885 and changed her name to Ruth Emilie Kaye, emigrating to

New South Wales, where she died in April 1944.

Dyer, Amelia (1895)

Amelia Dyer's sinister baby-farming activities emerged at her trial in 1896. Bristol-born Dyer, a mother and respected member of the Salvation Army, left her husband and started baby-farming in Long Ashton, but she was discovered, imprisoned, and remained in a workhouse until June 1895. She then moved to Reading, where she began to advertise herself as a child-minder in the local paper.

A public hanging at Newgate Prison, where Dyer was executed.

A Fatal Mistake

On 30 March 1895, a bargeman pulled a brown-paper parcel from the Thames and in it discovered the body of a baby girl. The child had been strangled with tape and a brick had been used to weigh the corpse down. On 2 April, a further two parcels were found stuffed into a carpet bag. Dyer – alias Mrs Thomas – had wrapped one of the children in brown paper that had her new name and address on it, and was arrested after two days. It became clear that many of the children barely lived 24 hours in Dyer's care.

The Reading Baby Farmer

Evidence against her appeared daily and four other corpses were fished out of the Thames. The 57-year-old became known as the Reading Baby Farmer. She attempted suicide, but failed and was put on trial. The defence claimed insanity, but the jury passed a guilty verdict and Dyer was hanged on 10 June 1896 after confessing her guilt.

See Elizabeth Brownrigg p. 124

Donald, Jeannie Ewan (1934)

Despite only circumstantial evidence, Jeannie Ewan Donald was found guilty of the murder of eight-year-old Helen Priestly on 16 July 1934. Helen disappeared in Aberdeen on 20 April whilst running an errand. The following day, a sack containing Helen's strangulated body was discovered in the tenement block. Someone had attempted to make the attack look like sexual assault, but investigations disproved this. Suspicion immediately fell on the Donalds, whose animosity towards the Priestly family was well known. Mr Donald was questioned but his alibi held and the police moved to Jeannie Donald, whose own alibi was disproved. After fibre, hair, blood and dust analysis tests had been conducted, Jeannie was arrested. The judge sentenced her to death, but this was commuted to life imprisonment; she was released on parole 10 years later.

Routier, Darlie Lynn (1996)

On 6 June 1996, Darlie Routier's young sons, Damon and Devon, were stabbed to death in their home in Rowlett, Texas. Routier told police that while she and her sons slept downstairs an unknown intruder had broken into their home and attacked her and the boys before escaping through the garage. Routier had been extensively injured during the attack and had to be hospitalized.

Claims of Innocence

Routier was arrested two weeks later and tried in 1997 in Kerrville because of pre-trial publicity in her own county. The jury convicted her of the murder of her son Damon, despite the stab wounds which she had suffered. She remains on death row, awaiting execution by lethal injection. Throughout the trial, and indeed since then, Routier has protested her innocence and has the continued support of her husband, Darin, who witnessed her injuries on that fateful night. Routier's defence attorneys believe that new forensic tests will help prove that she is innocent, including the blood on the nightshirt she was wearing, unknown fingerprints in the house and the presence of male pubic hair in the kitchen.

See Kristin Rossum p. 132

Poisoners

Poison seems to have been the murder weapon of choice for many female killers – particularly in the past. Arsenic, often readily available, has been a special favourite of women looking to dispatch their victims cleanly by means of poisoned food.

Blandy, Mary (1752)

One of the most famous crimes in eighteenth-century England was that of Mary Blandy and her married lover, Captain William Henry Cranstoun.

Mary Blandy (left) pictured with Elizabeth Jefferies, with whom she corresponded from prison.

MURDER FOR MONEY

Mary's father Francis was reputedly a man of wealth and although Cranstoun was already married, Francis offered him a dowry of £10,000 for his daughter. Mary and Cranstoun had their sights set higher than this, though, and planned to poison Francis and inherit all his money. They systematically fed arsenic to the old man, but their activities aroused suspicion and they were reported to the authorities.

The Twist in the Tale

Cranstoun fled to France, leaving Mary to face the trial alone. The case was heard at Oxford Assizes in February 1752 and Mary maintained that she believed the poison was simply a drug to make her father approve of her lover. Despite this, she was found guilty and faced execution on 6 April 1752. When her father's estate was settled, it was revealed that he was not even worth the £10,000 dowry he had offered.

Edmunds, Christiana (1871)

The case of Christiana Edmunds is one of unrequited love. In 1871, Christiana was a 42-year-old spinster living in Brighton, when she met and fell in love with Dr Beard, who was already married. Their relationship began with the exchange of passionate letters, but things soon became out of hand as Christiana endeavoured to poison Beard's wife by filling chocolate creams with strychnine. Beard suspected what was going on but, fearing a scandal, he simply forbade Christiana from seeing him.

Prolific poisoner Christiana Edmunds bought strychnine over the counter at a chemist's.

The Chocolate Cream Poisoner

Devastated by the end of the affair, Christiana embarked on a new career as the 'Chocolate Cream Poisoner'. She bought several more batches of chocolates, laced them with strychnine and then returned them to the shop. Over the next few weeks, several people fell seriously ill and when Sidney Barker died, Beard contacted the police and told them what he knew. Christiana was sent to Broadmoor, where she died in 1907.

See Jean Harris p. 138

Maybrick, Florence (1889)

Florence Maybrick, convicted of killing her husband in 1889.

James Maybrick, considered by many to be a Jack the Ripper suspect, met Florence, an Alabaman, onboard ship in March 1881. They married in July, despite the fact that James, a successful Liverpool cotton broker, was a habitual drug user with a mistress and several children.

When Maybrick became ill, the household nurse, Alice Yapp, and James's brothers, Edwin and Michael, became convinced that Florence was poisoning Maybrick, because she was known to use fly papers containing arsenic as a way of removing facial skin blemishes. On 11 May 1889, James lapsed into a coma and died. The post-mortem led to Florence's arrest, and the coroner's inquest in May of that year recommended that Florence be brought before the Liverpool Assizes.

Insubstantial Evidence?

Despite evidence that her husband had taken arsenic as well as other drugs, the jury was convinced of Florence's guilt and sentenced her to death. The public, however, demanded a reprieve. Finally, the Home Secretary transmuted her sentence to life imprisonment. Florence spent 15 years in prison, and was released in 1904. She died at the age of 79 whilst living as a recluse in Connecticut; she never accepted that her sentence was just.

See Alma Rattenbury p. 135

Creighton, Mary and Applegate, Everett (1936)

Mary Creighton may have been responsible for the deaths of three people, including her own brother. She and her husband John were arrested in 1923 after the death by poisoning of her brother Raymond. Creighton was the beneficiary of his estate, but she was acquitted of the charges. She was later arrested again on suspicion of the murder of her father-in-law, but again she was found not guilty.

In the 1930s, Mary and John and their daughter Ruth moved into the home of the Applegate family. Mary began an affair with Everett Applegate and used arsenic to poison his wife Ada in September 1936. Mary and Everett went on trial in January 1937 and they were both found guilty of murder. They were executed at Sing Sing Prison on 16 July 1937.

Wilson, Mary (1956)

Mary Wilson became known as the Widow of Windy Nook. Her 41-year marriage to husband John ended abruptly in July 1955. The Wilsons had taken in a lodger, John Russell, who was soon sharing Mary's bed. After poisoning her husband, Mary killed Russell in the same way in January 1956. She married Oliver Leonard in June the same year; he lasted just 13 days. Ernest Wilson did not do much better as he only lasted two weeks after their marriage the following year. Mary only inherited small sums of money from each of the men.

Ultimately, the police ordered the exhumation of the bodies and found a connection between them: they all contained rat poison and phosphorous. In the Leeds Assizes in March 1958, she claimed that her elderly husbands had taken phosphorous as an aphrodisiac. Unconvinced, the jury found her guilty and she remained in prison until her death on 5 December 1962.

Barber, Susan (1981)

Susan and Michael Barber lived with their three children in Westcliffe-on-Sea, Essex. On 31 March 1981, a cancelled fishing trip caused Michael to return home unexpectedly, where he discovered his 15-year-old friend Richard Collins in bed with his wife. He threw Collins out of the house and beat up his wife.

Paraquat Poisoning

Michael began suffering from headaches, nausea and stomach pains. Despite antibiotics, his condition worsened and he was admitted to Hammersmith Hospital; he died there on 27 June and was cremated a few days later. A suspicious pathologist had retained some of Michael's organs, however, and further tests revealed paraquat poisoning.

Susan was charged with murder, conspiracy to murder and administering poison, and Richard was charged with conspiracy. Susan admitted that she had put poison in gravy which only Michael ate. Richard received two years and Susan life imprisonment. In July 1983, Susan remarried in prison.

Rossum, Kristin (2002)

American Kristin Rossum was a toxicologist working in San Diego when she was convicted of murdering her husband Greg de Villers. She told the police that he had taken a combination of old prescription drugs she bought in Mexico while she was trying to kick her addiction to methamphetamine, or crystal meth. She claimed that Greg had taken his own life as he feared their marriage was near its end; when paramedics arrived at the scene following her 911 call, they found a wedding photo near to his body which was sprinkled with rose petals.

The Perfect Poison

Rossum had actually used fentanyl, an opiate given to cancer patients, 80 times more powerful than morphine. Fentanyl was the perfect poison: odourless, colourless and dissolvable. She may have conspired with her lover, Australian-born Michael Robertson, to kill Greg with drugs stolen from their office. They were both sacked when several doses were found to be missing after her husband's death. In December 2002, she was given life without parole.

See Forensic Entomology p. 242

Crimes of Passion

Hell hath no fury like a woman scorned... In these cases, the adage is true. Jealousy, despair, revenge, betrayal – all are causes for crimes of passion. The cases in this section reveal the lengths to which women will go when love turns to hate.

Pearcey, Mary (1890)

Mary Pearcey's house in Camden Town, where she murdered her lover's wife.

Mary Pearcey had been having an affair with the married Frank Hogg. On 23 October 1890, Mary invited Frank's wife Phoebe and their 18-month-old daughter to pay a visit to her house. Later that day, a Hampstead policeman found a woman's body lying amongst rubble; her skull had been crushed and her head severed from her body. A bloodstained pram was found nearby. On 25 October, the body of Frank Hogg's daughter was discovered; she had been suffocated.

The Evidence Revealed

The police learned of Mary's affair with Frank and a search of her house revealed a poker covered with hair and blood, and a bloodstained knife, as well as blood on the kitchen walls, ceiling and Mary's underwear. Throughout their search, Mary played her piano and sang. She denied seeing Phoebe on the day of the murder. Further investigation revealed that the child had been alive on leaving Mary's house, but had probably been suffocated by the weight of her mother's body when it was dumped into the pram.

The Final Word

Mary was tried at the Old Bailey, her defence claiming insanity, but the jury were unconvinced and she was hanged on 23 December at Newgate Prison. Mary's last request was for a mysterious advertisement to be placed in a Madrid newspaper, which read 'M.E.C.P. Last wish of M.E.W. Have not betrayed.'

See Yvonne Sleightholme p. 139

Gunness, Belle (1908)

Norwegian-born widow Belle Gunness lived in Laporte, Indiana, with her three children and her lover, Ray Lamphere. In a bizarre practice, Gunness advertised in the Chicago newspapers for suitors to share her farm. When they arrived at the farm in Indiana, they were drugged, robbed, butchered and buried. Fourteen men were killed in this way.

Local officials look through the remains of Belle Gunness's burned-down house.

Murderess or Victim?

When the farm went up in flames on 28 April 1908, investigators found the bodies of the three children and a headless female corpse, who they believed to be Gunness; the discovery of some dentures seemed to corroborate this. Lamphere was charged with the murder of Gunness and the children. In prison, he confided that they had lured an unknown woman to the farm, killed her and planted the dentures. Gunness had disappeared with the proceeds of the robberies and murders, never to be seen again.

See Mary Wilson p. 131

Rattenbury, Alma (1935)

In 1935, Britain was riveted by the Rattenbury Murder Case and the relationship between a woman in her mid-thirties and an 18-year-old chauffeur. It was all to end in great melodrama and tragedy.

Two Culprits

At 2 a.m. on Sunday 25 March 1935, police were called to the Rattenbury home in Bournemouth to find the distinguished Canadian architect Francis Rattenbury severely battered but still alive; he would die in hospital four days later. Alma immediately confessed, but so too did the chauffeur, George Stoner. They both then pleaded not guilty in court. Stoner was sentenced to hang but he refused to implicate Alma and she was cleared.

A local newspaper reports on the Rattenbury case.

Mystery Ending

Three days after the trial ended, Alma travelled to Christchurch. She then sat down by a river bank, wrote a note and stabbed herself six times. Her death released Stoner from his vow of silence and he recounted that both he and Alma had been upstairs when they heard a groan. They had come down to see Francis battered. His appeal was still turned down but he served just seven years, later becoming a distinguished soldier during the Second World War.

See Florence Maybrick p. 130

Beck, Martha (1948)

Martha Beck and Raymond Fernandez became known as the Lonely Hearts Killers. Beck was an overweight, highly sexed individual who had several disastrous relationships before meeting Fernandez through a lonely hearts advertisement.

Lonely Hearts Killings

During the 1940s, they began to prey on other lonely hearts, using Fernandez's charm to seduce the women and persuade them to hand over their savings. By December 1948, the deceptions turned to death, with the murder of Janet Fay and, shortly after, Delphine Downing and her young child.

Fay's body was found in New York and Beck and Fernandez were charged with three murders and linked to a further 17. In court, Beck was candid about her sexual relationship with Fernandez, providing sensational headlines. They were electrocuted on 8 March 1951 in Sing Sing Prison.

Raymond Fernandez (third from left) and Martha Beck in court, charged with three murders.

Ellis, Ruth (1955)

It was clear from the outset that Ruth Ellis was guilty of gunning down David Blakely at 9 p.m. on Easter Sunday, 10 April 1955. The possible motive, however, and the assistance of Desmond Cussen, were facts largely ignored by the court during her trial.

The Facts of the Case

Ellis and Blakely had met in 1953 at the Steering Wheel Club in Brick Street, near Hyde Park Corner, and for the next two years, they endured a tumultuous relationship, punctuated by

David Blakely, a racing driver, and Ruth Ellis, who murdered him in 1955.

bouts of violence, heavy drinking and overwhelming jealousy. In January 1955, Ellis fell pregnant with Blakely's child; he beat her and punched her in the stomach, causing her to miscarry. Although Ellis was certainly having an affair with Blakely's friend Desmond Cussen, the prospect of Blakely seeing another woman – as he had frequently threatened – was too much. On Easter Sunday, Ellis and Cussen drove Blakely to Hampstead and shot him. On the day before her execution, a statement showed that Cussen had provided the gun and taken her for gun practice in woods the day before the shooting. Ruth Ellis was hanged at Holloway Prison on 13 July 1955.

See Hanging p. 247

Garvie, Sheila (1968)

A complex sex life led to murder in Kincardineshire, Scotland, in 1968. Sheila Garvie found that her husband Maxwell's sexual demands were too overwhelming for her alone and in 1967, the couple began sharing their bed with Brian Tevendale and his sister Trudy. Brian and Sheila made plans to run away together, whilst Trudy, although married to an Aberdeen policeman, was quite content with Max. Nonetheless, Sheila and Brian murdered Max and his body was not found until mid-August – in an underground tunnel at Lauriston Castle.

Sheila and Brian were found guilty of murder and sentenced to life imprisonment. An accomplice, Alan Peters, received a verdict of not proven. Sheila had been turned in by her own mother after she had confided her part in the murders.

Harris, Jean (1980)

Jean Harris, the headmistress of an exclusive Virginian girls' school, murdered her lover, Dr Herman Tarnower, the creator of the Scarsdale Diet. Jealousy of Tarnower's affairs compelled Harris to drive for five hours in the rain to his home in Westchester, New York, and to shoot him four times on 10 March 1980. She had intended to shoot herself, but instead, she lived and was convicted of murder and sentenced to 15 years in prison. Harris was addicted to amphetamines and she claimed that she felt suicidal whilst suffering from withdrawal symptoms at the time of the murder. Harris wrote three books in prison and suffered two heart attacks, but in 1992 she was released and has subsequently become a prison reformer.

See Ruth Ellis p. 137

Sleightholme, Yvonne (1988)

When William Smith ended his 18-month relationship with Yvonne Sleightholme, she told him she was suffering from leukaemia and the guilt-ridden William took her back.

A Woman Scorned

Yvonne began planning their wedding, innocent of the fact that William had rekindled a relationship with a former lover, Jayne Wilford. Yvonne moved out when William told her he was to marry Jayne in May 1988. Soon after, the couple began receiving threatening phone calls, suffered arson attacks on their farm and were sent a wreath. The police were called in, but nothing came of their investigations.

Jean Harris arrives at court, charged with Dr Herman Tarnower's murder.

On 13 December, Yvonne shot Jayne in the head and feigned a sexual attack on her. The police investigated Yvonne's relationship with William and carried out forensic tests on her car, positively identifying Jayne's blood on the upholstery. On 10 May 1991, Yvonne Sleightholme was jailed for life at Leeds Crown Court.

Philpott, Gillian (1989)

Twenty-one-year-old Gillian Philpott's new husband, Graham, was a 45-year-old divorced father of three, as well as being her boss at the bank where she worked. Gillian's twin sister, Janet, accompanied them on their honeymoon and later lodged with them.

Suicide Pact or Murder?

By December 1989, Gillian was convinced that her sister and her husband were having an affair and confronted them; Janet left the house. At New Year, a drunken Graham asked for a divorce; Gillian's response was to strangle him with a dressing-gown cord. She tried to make it look like suicide by faking a note, before attempting to kill herself by driving her car to the edge of a cliff. The car pitched over, but Gillian only sustained superficial injuries.

She was found guilty of manslaughter in January 1991 and was sentenced to two years. Despite attempts to fake a suicide pact, forensic evidence pointed to murder.

Broderick, Betty (1989)

Betty was born to devout Roman Catholic parents in New York State, USA. She married Daniel T. Broderick III in 1969 and the couple had five children. Betty supported Dan and their family while he trained to be a lawyer. The family moved to San Diego, where Dan's career took off and he eventually became a multi-millionaire. Despite their affluent lifestyle, Dan and Betty's marriage deteriorated and Dan began an affair with his assistant, Linda. After Betty found out about the affair, the couple were rancorously divorced in 1989 and three months later Dan married Linda. After Dan's lawyers threatened Betty with contempt over the custody battle, she went to Dan's home and shot her ex-husband and his new wife.

A Difficult Case to Try

Betty was tried twice; the first trial ended in a hung jury. In a second trial, she was convicted of two counts of second degree murder. The jury foreman said after the trial: 'We only wondered what took her so long to kill him.' She was sentenced in 1991 to 32 years; in 2010 she was denied parole for at least another 15 years.

See Yvonne Sleightholme p. 139

Gluzman, Rita (1996)

On the morning of 7 April 1996, a New Jersey police patrolman spotted a man taking bags out of the boot of two cars and throwing them into the river. He decided to investigate and found eight other bags. The bags contained blood-soaked clothing and parts of a body later identified as Yakov Gluzman. He had been cut into 65 pieces using hacksaws and a scalpel; his fingertips had been removed in an attempt to hide his identity. The policeman arrested the man, Vladimir Zelenin, on the spot.

Emigrating to the USA

Rita and her infant son had emigrated from the former Soviet Union as part of the Jewish exodus in the late 1960s; her husband had not been permitted a visa and so had remained in the USSR. On reaching the US Rita had campaigned tirelessly on her husband's behalf, and in 1971 he was finally granted a visa and was at last able to join his family.

Plotting Murder

Gluzman continued his work as a molecular biologist, and rose to a prominent position in a leading research laboratory; he and Rita also set up a computer company together. They epitomized the American dream, and became millionaires. However, their marriage was failing and in 1995 Gluzman filed for divorce on the grounds of mental cruelty. The divorce was acrimonious and in March of that year she approached Zelenin, her cousin, to help her kill Yakov. Knowing her husband's movements and having a key to his apartment allowed them to ambush, murder and dismember him. Zelenin had struck the first blow and Rita had finished Yakov off, beginning the dismemberment herself.

Domestic Violence First

When Zelenin was interviewed, he readily implicated Rita, but she had disappeared. When she was eventually caught, she was charged under the 1994 Domestic Violence Statute, until that time never used against a woman. There was no physical evidence tying her to the crime, yet she was sentenced to life imprisonment. In 1999, the US Supreme Court refused to hear Rita Gluzman's appeal.

6

juvenile killers

Parent-Killers

Just as parents can turn murderous towards their children, so children can inexplicably kill their parents. The question uppermost in the public's mind in such cases is whether these children were born evil or if in fact the parents were to blame for their own fate.

Borden, Lizzie (1892)

Young Lizzie Borden was convinced that her father's new wife, Abby, had married him for his money. On the morning of 4 August 1892, Bridget Sullivan, the maid at their home in Fall River, Massachusetts, was awoken by Lizzie's cries that someone had killed her father.

Getting Away with Murder?

When the police arrived, they immediately questioned Lizzie about her movements prior to her parents' deaths. She was forced to stand trial in June 1893. There was only circumstantial evidence against Lizzie, but she had become a wealthy young lady on the death of her father and stepmother. However, the jury at her trial were told: 'To find her guilty, you must believe she is a fiend. Gentlemen, does she look like it?' The jury clearly did not think so and found her not guilty. Lizzie died in 1927, but not before Bridget had retired to Ireland, with a sizeable chunk of the fortune.

Mass-poisoner Graham Young, who was found guilty in 1972.

Young, Graham (1962–72)

From an early age, Graham Young had been fascinated with poisons and with death. He became an avid reader of accounts of the Moors Murders and of Adolf Hitler's activities.

Early Experiments

He began experimenting with poison on his family at the age of 13, trying out belladonna on his sister, Winifred. Mercifully, the dose was insufficient to kill her; Young claimed he had put it in her tea by mistake.

Throughout 1962, several members of the Young family fell ill, as did a school friend of Graham's. At Easter that year, his stepmother Molly died. His father took a turn for the worse and hospital tests showed arsenic and antimony poisoning. Young was sent to Broadmoor. He spent nine years there and, on his release, he began his new life working in Hertfordshire.

Young Frankenstein

In November 1971, two of his workmates died of thallium poisoning and two more were seriously ill from the effects of Young's experiments with poisons. Young described himself as 'your friendly neighbourhood Frankenstein' and the police were well aware of his criminal background. Young, always an outsider, verbally vicious and willing to turn to poison if someone crossed him, was sentenced to life in 1972.

Sherman, Timothy Scott (1987)

Early in the morning of 12 October 1987, Ann and Stevenson Sherman were shot and killed while asleep in their bed. When the police arrived, the Shermans' 18-year-old son Timothy was in the house with his maternal grandfather, William Gibson. Timothy told the officers that he had heard gunshots and had run to his grandfather's nearby home. The two of them returned to the Sherman house, where Gibson called the police.

Teenage Gunman

In Timothy's bedroom, police discovered a box of 12-gauge shotgun shells stuffed under the mattress of his bed. Two shells were missing. As well as the shotgun shells the hidden gun was also found and had Timothy's fingerprints on it. In 1988, a Maryland jury convicted Sherman of killing his mother and adoptive father, and sentenced him to two consecutive life terms.

Child Attacks

Children with the killing instinct will usually turn to other children when in search of victims, especially those younger, weaker and more vulnerable than they are. What starts as bullying behaviour before adolescence has been seen to turn into murderous intent in teenage years.

Schneider, Marie (1886)

From an early age, Marie Schneider showed signs of extreme disobedience and a tendency to bully other children so she could steal from them. As she grew older, however, she also acquired a taste for torturing them. In 1886, at the age of just 12, Marie took the final step and committed murder. She took a three-year-old girl to the second storey of a building and, after stealing her earrings, ordered her to sit on the windowsill. Marie then pushed the child to her death. Apparently, she wanted to sell the earrings so she could buy sweets. She was sentenced to eight years imprisonment.

See Jesse Pomeroy p. 150

The late–nineteenth–century outskirts of Berlin, where Marie Schneider lived.

Bell, Mary and Bell, Norma (1968)

In May 1968, three children stumbled upon the corpse of youngster Martin Brown. A few days after Martin's death, someone broke into his nursery school and scribbled on a wall in crayon, 'I murder so that I may come back'. Handwriting experts were sure it was the work of a child.

The Two Bells

In August 1968, three-year-old Brian Howe was found strangled near the same school and the Newcastle police began interviewing all of its 1,200 underage residents. The police made two arrests based on their enquiries: Mary Bell and Norma Bell; although neighbours, the two 11-year-olds were not related. During interviews, each accused the other of 'squeezing' Brian Howe's throat, but both denied having anything to do with the murder of Martin Brown.

'We All Die'

The girls were tried in December 1968. Mary bragged in court that she wrote the graffiti 'for giggles' and confidently stated that 'murder isn't that bad ... we all die someday anyway'. Norma was quieter and seemed more fragile; she was to receive three years' probation. Mary was sent to a detention centre, then prison, and was released in 1980 at the age of 23.

Child killer Mary Bell, who was released from prison in 1980.

Thompson, Robert and Venables, Jon (1993)

On 12 February 1993, 10-year-olds Robert Thompson and Jon Venables murdered James Bulger – who was just two years old – in a case that shocked the nation.

Murder on the Tracks

The two boys had found James playing inside a shopping centre in Liverpool, while his mother was in a shop. They took him on a long walk that ended at the railway tracks. Here, they splashed him with blue paint, then battered him with bricks and an iron bar. He was still alive, so they draped him over the train track and waited for the inevitable. There was also evidence that the child was sexually abused.

Police restrain a man from throwing a rock at the van carrying James Bulger's killers.

Arrest, Imprisonment and Release

On 18 February, Thompson and Venables were arrested and subsequently charged with murder, after Venables broke down during interview and admitted his part in the killing. It was to be several years before Thompson confessed his guilt.

Thompson and Venables were granted release on parole in 2001, after being provided with new identities. They had spent just eight years, four months and 10 days in secure local care homes, a few miles from the Bulger home, for the horrific murder. In 2010, it was revealed that Venables had been imprisoned again for offences linked to violations of his release licence.

The West Memphis Three (1993)

On 5 May 1993, three eight-year-old boys left the Weaver Elementary School, near West Memphis, Arkansas, after an ordinary day. They were never seen alive again. The following afternoon, their bodies were found in a creek area known as Robin Hood Hills; they were naked and had been beaten and tied. One had been repeatedly stabbed in the groin and then castrated. Police believed that the deaths were the result of some bizarre satanic ritual and already knew of a boy who was interested in such things – Damien Echols.

A Controversial Case

There was no evidence to connect Echols to the crime, yet he and his two friends, Jason Baldwin and Jessie Misskelley, were tried and found guilty of the murders, primarily the result of the testimony of a local woman who was determined to earn a reward. She told her son to say that he had seen Echols in the area and approached Misskelley, a 17-year-old mentally impaired boy, to fabricate an eyewitness account. The police manipulated his evidence, which served to corroborate their suspicions, but by fabricating the account, Misskelley incriminated both Baldwin and himself. The three young men are still in prison, fighting for a fair retrial.

Tate, Lionel (1999)

Lionel Tate was just 12 when he was indicted for the murder of six-year-old Tiffany Eunick. Two years later, a jury found him guilty of first-degree murder, a conviction which, in Florida, carries a sentence of either execution or life without parole.

Just Playing

The murder took place on 28 July 1999, when Tiffany was taken to the home of childminder Kathleen Gossett-Tate for the night. Kathleen went to bed at 10 p.m. Forty minutes later, Tiffany was dead; she showed evidence of 32 different injuries, consistent with punching, kicking and other physical violence.

Had Tate admitted to the attacks, he would have received three years and a period of probation, but he chose not to and was sentenced to life. His mother Kathleen said, 'How do you accept a plea for second-degree murder when your child was just playing?'

Teenage Terror

In modern times, the rise in incidences of young people committing all manner of crimes – even murder – is often blamed on the violence they encounter on television, in films and video games. But teenage killers have been around for centuries.

Pomeroy, Jesse (1871-74)

Jesse Pomeroy started his reign of terror in the Boston area of the United States at the tender age of 12. Between December 1871 and February 1872, he abducted, tortured and probably raped several young boys. He was quickly identified and sentenced to an 18-month spell in a reform school. He was released in February 1874, but it seems he had not learnt his lesson.

Two Deaths

In April of that year, a young girl, Mary Curran, disappeared, quickly followed by four-year-old Horace Mullen. When police found Horace's body, it showed around 30 stab wounds and the head had almost been severed. The subsequent investigation uncovered a blood-stained knife and muddy shoes in Pomeroy's room; Curran's decomposed body was later found in the cellar.

Boston's Old State House around the time of the Jesse Pomeroy killings.

Prison Life

On 10 December 1874, Pomeroy was sentenced to death, but as he was only 14, this was commuted to solitary imprisonment for life. In 1883, after fracturing a gas pipe, Pomeroy blew open his cell door; he was seriously injured and three other prisoners were killed. Pomeroy died, still incarcerated, at the age of 72. Despite claims at the time that he had murdered up to 27 children, it seems likely that Curran and Mullen were his only two killings, although he was certainly guilty of numerous assaults and rapes.

See Marie Schneider p. 146

Leopold, Nathan and Loeb, Richard (1924)

Nathan Leopold and Richard Loeb, law students at the University of Chicago, wanted to commit the perfect crime. It was the summer of 1924 and the two bored young men hired a car under false names and drove to a private school, where they offered 14-year-old Robert Franks a ride. They had written a ransom note even before knowing who they would kidnap, and this was delivered to Franks' distraught father, Jacob, the following morning. Before Franks could deliver the $10,000 ransom that afternoon, the body of his son was found in a culvert 30 km (20 miles) south of Chicago.

Nathan Leopold and Richard Loeb, kidnappers and murderers, are escorted by police.

Accidental Death

Near the corpse was a pair of spectacles that were quickly linked to Leopold. The boys' alibi was flimsy and they broke down and confessed to the murder. Loeb claimed that he had intended to knock Franks unconscious with a chisel, but the blow had been too hard. A bloodstained rental car was retrieved, Loeb's typewriter matched the ransom note and the spectacles provided irrefutable evidence. The boys' defence counsel entered a plea of guilty on the grounds of temporary insanity to reduce the sentence from mandatory execution to a prison sentence. Loeb died in prison in 1936 and Leopold was released in 1958.

See Serology p. 239

McDonald, Roland (1924)

Fifteen-year-old Roland McDonald from Amhurst, Maine, was convicted of shooting schoolteacher Louise Gerrish in 1924. After 34 years in prison, he took a lie-detector test that suggested he may have been innocent after all. Nonetheless, his parole request was turned down. In many countries, the treatment of juvenile offenders was as harsh as that of adults; they were expected to display the same degree of maturity.

See Lie Detectors and Polygraphs p. 245

Collier, Cindy and Wolf, Shirley (1983)

Cindy Collier (15) and Shirley Wolf (14) used their youth and gender to con their way into peoples' California apartments in order to rob them. They knocked on doors at random and on one occasion, an elderly woman, Anna Brackett, let them in and they chatted to her for a while, planning how best to steal her belongings. Suddenly, Wolf grabbed the woman by the neck and Collier ran into the kitchen and brought in a knife. Wolf then stabbed Anna Brackett 28 times. The killers were soon picked up by the police and they openly confessed that they had enjoyed killing the woman and would undoubtedly kill again. They were given the maximum sentence for children of their ages and were both released at the age of 27.

Tackett, Laurie and Loveless, Melinda (1992)

On the night of 10 January 1992, lesbians Melinda Loveless (16), Laurie Tackett (17), Hope Rippey (15) and Toni Lawrence (15) abducted and murdered 12-year-old Shanda Sharer in Madison, Indiana. Shanda had been dating Loveless's former girlfriend, Amanda Heavrin. They took her to an abandoned house, where they tortured her and then threw her into the back of a car, hitting her with a tyre iron every time she made a noise. They then drove her to another isolated spot, where they poured petrol over her, setting her on fire while she was still alive.

Trial and Sentence

The girls were quickly identified and Loveless pleaded guilty to murder, arson and imprisonment, and was sentenced to 60 years. Tackett received the same sentence. Rippey was given 60 years, with 10 years suspended and 10 years of probation. Lawrence, less active in the torture and murder, was given 20 years. In November 1998, Lawrence was eligible for an early release, but the parole board turned down her request. She was finally paroled in December 2000.

Zamora, Diane and Graham, David (1995)

Teenagers Diane Zamora and David Graham started dating in August 1995, but in November of that year, Graham was unfaithful to Diane. When he confessed his infidelity, Diane told him he must kill the girl he had betrayed her with, Adrianne Jones.

On 3 December, in their home town of Grand Prairie, Texas, David arranged a date with Adrianne. Together, they drove out to a secluded spot where Diane, hidden in the car, smashed her victim's head in with a dumbbell.

Life Sentence

The body was found the next day and David was interviewed and cleared, but in August the following year, Diane confessed to two friends, who promptly contacted the authorities. On 17 February 1998, Diane was convicted and received a life sentence. In July of that year, David was also convicted and sentenced to life. Neither will be eligible for parole for 40 years.

Ferrell, Roderick (1996)

Roderick Ferrell, aged 16, from Murray in Kentucky, led a vampire clan whose members often cut their arms open to suck each other's blood. One day, Ferrell led the group to Eustis in Florida, where he killed the elderly parents of a former girlfriend, Heather Wendorf. Heather had remained with two other girls while Ferrell took Howard Scott Anderson with him to the Wendorf home. Inside, he clubbed the sleeping Richard Wendorf with a crowbar and then stabbed Naoma to death. On Richard's chest, Ferrell burned the shape of a 'V' with some cigarettes.

The Fates of the Vampires

The others implicated in the attack, Dana Cooper and Charity Keesee, were sentenced to imprisonment. Cooper will be released in 2014; Keesee is already out of prison. Ferrell and Anderson are serving life sentences. Heather was cleared of all charges. In March 2003, Ferrell began a request for a retrial, claiming he had an inadequate defence in 1996.

See Luke Woodham p. 157

Tulloch, Robert and Parker, James (2001)

In February 2001, teenagers Robert Tulloch and James Parker were charged with the murders of husband-and-wife Dartmouth College professors, Half and Susanne Zantop. The stabbings had taken place in Hanover, Vermont, on 27 January 2001. They were arrested at an Indiana truck stop two days after fleeing Vermont, where they had voluntarily given fingerprints.

Random Murders

In the six months before the murders took place, Tulloch and Parker went to four other randomly chosen homes, planning to talk their way in, find the residents' ATM cards and PIN numbers and then murder them. According to friends and neighbours, the pair did everything together – and that included murder, it seems. A fingerprint found on a knife sheath left at the scene matched Parker's, and bloody footprints also linked Tulloch to the crime. In April 2002, they were both sentenced to life.

See Cindy Collier and Shirley Wolf p. 152

James Parker js led to the Henry County Courthouse, suspected of killing two professors.

School Attacks

In recent years, there have been increasing incidences of school shootings, especially in the USA. Frustrated, lonely, angry, rejected ... these teenage spree killers often choose their school as the place to vent their rage. Armed with guns, these are the kids that every parent, teacher and fellow student fears.

Spencer, Brenda (1979)

Brenda Spencer was the inspiration for the Boomtown Rats' hit single 'I Don't Like Mondays', as this was, in her own words, the reason why she murdered two people and wounded nine others on a Monday morning in January 1979.

Spencer was just 16 at the time, but had been given a rifle and considerable amounts of ammunition by her father as a Christmas present. Spencer was an epileptic and suffered from bouts of depression. In court, she blamed her father for having sexually abused her for several years.

Monday Morning Blues

Her home was across the street from San Diego's Grover Cleveland Elementary School. She shot the principal and another male worker at the school, then wounded eight pupils and a police officer who tried to intervene. She pleaded guilty to murder and assault and was sentenced to two life sentences. Spencer remains in prison and, to this day, is considered a threat.

PRESENTED BY THE STUDENT BODY
IN MEMORY OF
BURTON WRAGG & MIKE SUCHA
WHO DIED IN THE SERVICE OF HELPING OTHERS
JANUARY 29, 1979

The memorial stone commemorating the victims of Brenda Spencer's shooting spree.

Loukaitis, Barry (1996)

Barry Loukaitis entered his classroom at Moses Lake, Washington, on 2 February 1996 dressed as a western gunfighter. The 14-year-old had two pistols, a high-powered rifle and nearly 80 rounds of ammunition. He shot and killed three and wounded several others; he then took hostages. The siege was finally ended when a teacher disarmed him.

Killing for Fun

Although Loukaitis claimed that he had been suffering from severe mood swings, one of his classmates told the police that Loukaitis had told him it would be fun to kill and that it was all planned. According to eyewitnesses, Loukaitis had shot without any emotion, apparently choosing targets at random in the class. Loukaitis was found guilty on all counts and sentenced to spend the rest of his life in prison.

See Dylan Klebold and Eric Harris p. 160

Woodham, Luke (1997)

On 1 October 1997, youngster Luke Woodham slit his mother's throat, then concealed a rifle in his coat and drove to Pearl High School in Mississippi. He opened fire on his school friends, killing two and wounding seven.

The Woodham family home, where Luke Woodham allegedly murdered his mother.

The Croth Cult

Woodham was a member of an adolescent demonic cult called 'Croth', and the other six boys in the group were charged with conspiring to help Woodham carry out the attack. Woodham claimed that he was under the spell of one of the others, Grant Boyette, who had caused him to be possessed by demons. On 5 June 1998, however, Woodham was found guilty of murdering his mother and sentenced to life. On 13 June, he was given two further life sentences and 20 years for the murder of two of his classmates.

See Roderick Ferrell p. 154

Carneal, Michael (1997)

At the age of just 14, Michael Carneal murdered three of his fellow students and wounded five others when he opened fire in a morning prayer meeting at Heath High School in Paducah, Kentucky, on 1 December 1997. He was armed with a handgun, two rifles, two shotguns and plenty of ammunition that he had stolen from a neighbour's garage. He had

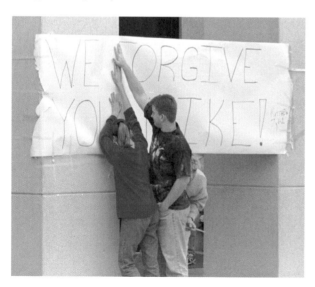

warned friends that something big was going to happen, but the young atheist, who had been the victim of bullying, had not disclosed his intentions.

Carneal pleaded guilty and was sentenced to be detained in a juvenile centre on the grounds of mental illness. In August 2000, the families of the three girls he killed agreed to a $42 million settlement, setting a legal precedent for school shootings in America.

Following the Kentucky shooting, students hang a poster reading 'WE FORGIVE YOU MIKE!'

See Dylan Klebold and Eric Harris p. 160

Golden, Andrew and Johnson, Mitchell (1998)

On 24 March 1998, cousins Mitchell Johnson (13) and Andrew Golden (11), dressed in camouflage gear, opened fire from woodland near their school in Jonesboro, Arkansas, while their classmates were engaged in a fake fire drill initiated by the two boys.

In a few brief moments, they had gunned down 12-year olds Natalie Brooks, Paige Ann Herring and Stephanie Johnson and 11-year-old Brittany Varner. Ten other pupils were wounded and a teacher, Shannon Wright, later died from her injuries. Significantly, all the victims were female; Johnson and Golden's targets were girls who had refused to date them. One of the wounded was Johnson's 11-year-old former girlfriend, Candace Porter, who had broken up with him the previous day.

Release on Attaining Adulthood

In court, both the boys were found guilty of murder and attempted murder, but under Arkansas law they could only be tried as juveniles, which meant they were both released when they reached 21. Johnson's lawyers claimed that their client had become disturbed since he had been molested at the age of six, whilst Golden's defence was a plea of insanity.

See Charles Whitman p. 46

Kinkel, Kipland (1998)

On 20 May 1998, 15-year-old Kipland Kinkel was expelled from Thurston High School in Springfield, Oregon, for having brought a loaded gun into class. That night, he murdered his own parents, booby-trapped the house with bombs, stole a car and the following morning, drove to school, heavily armed

High–school killer Kipland Kinkel in a photograph of his fifth grade football team.

with a rifle, two handguns, a knife and pepper spray. Kinkel walked into the school cafeteria and indiscriminately opened fire. The attack was only brought to a halt when a wounded student forced Kinkel to the ground. Two students were killed and 22 others were wounded as a result of the attack. It was amazing that so few had been hit or killed – over 400 people were in the cafeteria when Kinkel opened fire.

Nature not Nurture

Kinkel came from a privileged background, yet had developed an interest in bomb-making and killing small animals; he was also an expert marksman. Even after his arrest, when he was being searched, Kinkel tried to stab a police officer and use his pepper spray. Kinkel was sentenced to 112 years in prison. In 2007, he was transferred to an adult prison.

Klebold, Dylan and Harris, Eric (1999)

Dylan Klebold and Eric Harris became known as the 'Trench Coat Mafia' and were responsible for a horrific attack on the Columbine High School in Littleton, Colorado, on 20 April 1999. Klebold was 17 and Harris 18. They revelled in everything German and were obsessed with the Nazis. There were eight other members of the Trench Coat Mafia, all of whom listened to Goth-rock music, wore swastikas, believed in white supremacy and considered themselves to be suburban terrorists.

The Columbine Massacre

The attack began at 11.30 a.m. and they rampaged through the school for four hours, combing the classrooms and corridors in a systematic manner, seeking out victims in a hideous version of hide-and-seek. Students and teachers hid wherever they could. In total, they slaughtered 12 students and a teacher, and wounded 24 others, five of whom were critically injured. When several SWAT teams arrived on the scene in an attempt to bring the attack to an end, the two boys turned the guns on themselves in the library. They left 50 explosive devices around the school and in their cars and homes.

See Barry Loukaitis p. 157

A girl puts 13 crosses into the ground to signify the victims of the Columbine shooting.

Williams, Charles Andrew (2001)

Charles Andrew Williams was just 15 years old when he launched his own mini version of the Columbine massacre. He had suffered from bullying and hated the discipline enforced at the Santana High School in Santee, California. The attack took place on 1 March 2001 and at the end of it, two students were dead, 11 were wounded and two teachers had also been seriously injured.

Williams was charged with two counts of murder and 26 counts of attempted murder; he is currently being held in a juvenile facility. Under Californian law, he will be eligible for parole at the age of 65. Had he been tried as a juvenile, he would have been released at the age of 25.

7

organized|crime

Gangs

These are the organizations that dominate the criminal underworld – a world peopled by powerful families that trade in drugs, launder money and run rackets. Out of these groups have risen some of the most infamous mob bosses of all time.

The Mafia (1880s-present)

Giuseppe Esposito was the first known Sicilian Mafia member to emigrate to the United States. Together with six other Sicilians, he fled to New York after murdering 11 wealthy landowners. He was arrested in New Orleans in 1881 and extradited back to Italy.

Turf Wars

The US Mafia was dominated by the Black Hand Gangs around 1900 and then the Five Points Gang in New York until Al Capone's syndicate, based in Chicago, took over in the 1920s. By the end of this decade, two factions had emerged, sparking off a turf war in New York. The murder of Joseph Masseria, one of the faction leaders, united the Mafia and it became La Cosa Nostra (LCN).

Salvatore Maranzano, the first leader, was murdered within six months and Charles 'Lucky' Luciano became the new head. Maranzano had established the Cosa Nostra code of conduct, set up the family divisions and structure, and established procedures for resolving disputes. Luciano continued his work by setting up the Commission, which controlled all La Cosa Nostra activities, run by bosses from six or seven families.

Mafia boss Lucky Luciano celebrates after being cleared of complicity in an international dope ring

The LCN Today

Today, the LCN is involved in corruption, drug trafficking, extortion, gambling, labour racketeering, loan sharking, murder, prostitution, pornography, stock manipulation schemes and tax fraud.

See Salvatore Maranzano p. 170

Murder, Incorporated (1935)

Murder, Incorporated was a contract killing gang run by Louis 'Lepke' Buchalter and Albert Anastasia. They limited their targets to those in the mob, such as Bugsy Siegel, Dutch Schultz and the New York district attorney Thomas E. Dewey. In October 1935, Mendy Weiss and Charles 'The Bug' Workman, two of Murder, Inc.'s most notorious killers, walked into the Palace Chop House and Tavern in Newark, New Jersey, and shot three of Schultz's men and then Schultz himself in the stomach. It has been estimated that over a period of 10 years, Murder, Inc. was responsible for between 500 and 700 murders from California to Connecticut.

See Bugsy Siegel p. 169

The New Mafia Order Today (2010)

The New Mafia Order, or the 'sistema', which has ruled Sicily for decades, has grown into a transnational empire of crime and now has power across the world beyond its wildest dreams.

Global Spread of the Sistema

The Mafia's control now extends beyond La Cosa Nostra and the Neapolitan Camorra, and incorporates organizations based in Turkey and Russia. The scope of the sistema includes Colombian cocaine cartels and their operations in Spain, as well as triad gangs in Asia (active in London and Rotterdam) and organized gangs of Albanians, Nigerians, Lebanese, Moroccans, Pakistanis and former Yugoslavs.

Back in the homeland, Palermo launders some $20 billion per year; the city is eightieth in Italy in terms of per capita income, but fifth in consumer spending, attesting to the fact that it is awash with Mafia money.

The Triads Today (2010)

Triad societies date back to the seventeenth century and have dominated the Chinese underworld for centuries. They base their organizations on secret rules and rituals, a sworn brotherhood built on kinship. They are actively involved in smuggling, drug trafficking, prostitution and other criminal activities, using fear and intimidation rather than violence.

Triad societies occur wherever there is a Chinese community. Hong Kong was at the very centre of their operations for many years, but latterly, they have turned their attention to China itself. They are active across the world to a greater or lesser extent, having established a presence in Chinese communities in a number of countries over the years.

Triad Links

The Triads have key connections in the United States, particularly California and New York, and in such European capitals as Amsterdam and London, but there is little prospect of the West being overrun by Triad gangs. Police estimate there are as many as 50 Triad societies in Hong Kong, the largest being the Wo Sing Wo and 14-K. Southern China and Hong Kong still represent their greatest sources of revenue.

Yardies (2010)

The term 'Yardie' is used to refer to Jamaicans who have just arrived from their home country (referred to as the 'back yard'). A typical Yardie is a single male, age 18–35, usually but not exclusively of Jamaican origin, many of whom have false identities or are known only by their street names. Great Britain and lately the United States are attractive destinations for Yardies, as they can more easily be assimilated into the West Indian populations.

Yardie Activities

Yardies are predominantly interested in drug trafficking and dealing and are renowned for their extreme violence. The US has made it increasingly difficult for Jamaican criminals to gain entry into the country, and consequently, Britain has become a staging ground to illegally obtain passports, making international movement easier.

Internal Warfare

Yardies tend to deal in the production and distribution of cocaine and are usually well armed. Jamaican crime groups have relatively small, flat organizations, making a rise to power easy if the individual has access to a drug supply and is prepared to protect his business. As a consequence, inter-Yardie warfare is commonplace and they are not averse to using firearms to deal with trivial disputes. Yardie gangs frequently break up and reorganize, which causes temporary chaos and conflict.

The Red Mafia Today (2010)

Russian organized crime is becoming a considerable concern, not only in Russia and the former Russian states, but in the rest of Europe and the US. The Red Mafia is actively involved in extortion, prostitution, fraud, car theft, counterfeiting, credit-card forgery, drug trafficking, money laundering and murder. An estimated 80 per cent of the private enterprises and commercial banks in Russia's major cities pay a tribute of 10–20 per cent of their profits to organized crime. During the 1970s and 1980s, it is believed that some 200,000 Russian citizens emigrated to the United States alone, a fair proportion of them unwanted Russian criminals.

Russian Gangs

It is estimated that some 5,000 Russian gangs operate in that country alone, with a membership of some 100,000. Each gang is run by a 'pakhan', who controls four cells through an intermediary called a 'brigadier'. The pakhan uses spies to ensure the brigadiers remain loyal. Regular members of the gang are unaware of the identity of their pakhan, but all strategy is decided by the pakhan and his closest associates.

Gang Codes

The members are bound by 18 codes, by which they live or die – breaking one of the codes is punishable by death. The Russian Mafia is technically advanced and has counter-intelligence groups and access to the latest equipment and intelligence.

See The Mafia p. 164

Gangs of New York

When the Mafia spread from its Sicilian origins, New York was the place in which it most obviously manifested. By the early years of the twentieth century, mobsters were engaged in all manner of criminal activity and turf wars. Even today, gang activity is rife on the streets of New York.

Costello, Frank (1916-57)

Frank Costello was born in Italy in 1891 and emigrated with his family to the United States as a child. As he grew up, he turned to petty crime and spent his teen years in and out of prison.

The Prime Minister

In 1916, Costello teamed up with gang leader Lucky Luciano and ran his bootlegging and gambling operations. He also nurtured his connections with politicians. His networking and contacts earned him the nickname the 'Prime Minister'. When Luciano was imprisoned in 1936, he chose Costello to run the business, with Vito Genovese as his second-in-command. By 1951, however, Genovese had planned to oust Costello and take over leadership of the gang himself.

Prison Time

Costello avoided death at this time, as he was sentenced to 14 months in prison for contempt of court; he was released in October 1953. He received another prison term in 1956, spending a further year inside. In 1957,

Frank Costello puffs on a cigarette as he leaves court following his testimony.

Costello survived a murder attempt by Vincent Gigante and was slightly wounded. Genovese appointed himself boss all the same. Costello was a practical man – he saw that Genovese had effective control of the mob and that he was always going to be a target for murder.

Costello agreed to retire; he gave up all his interests and promised never to be involved in the business again. He was true to his word and passed away peacefully in a Manhattan hospital in 1975.

Lucky Luciano (1920–36)

Luciano was born in Sicily in 1896. His family moved to America in 1906, settling in New York. He was arrested in 1915 for heroin dealing and given a prison term. In 1920, he joined Joe Masseria's gang and had risen to under-boss by 1925. Luciano was nearly killed in the war that broke out between Masseria and Salvatore Maranzano, earning him the nickname 'Lucky'.

King of New York

In April 1931, Luciano was involved in the murders of Masseria and Maranzano, which made him the undisputed boss of New York. He was instrumental in the formation of Murder, Incorporated to enforce mob law.

Imprisonment and Extradition

In 1936, he was sentenced to 30 years, but was released in 1946 for his assistance during the war and deported to Italy. He died in Naples on 26 January 1962.

Siegel, Bugsy (1920s–47)

Bugsy Siegel was born in Brooklyn in 1906. He teamed up with Meyer Lansky and became involved in bootlegging. By the late 1920s, he had joined the gang led by Joe Masseria. In 1937, Siegel went to California to develop gambling ships, operating outside the jurisdiction of the authorities. Siegel's partners in New York suspected that he was hiding some of the profits and on 20 June 1947, he was murdered in his Beverly Hills home.

Gambino, Carlo (1920s–50s)

Carlo Gambino was born in Sicily in 1902 into a gangster family. He worked as a hit man

during his teens, and in the early 1920s, he went to the United States to join forces with his cousins, the Castellanos. During the period of Prohibition, he worked as a gunman, driver and bootlegger, and became an associate of mob leader Lucky Luciano. He also married Paul Castellano's sister.

The Godfather

By the 1950s, Albert Anastasia had become the head of the family, but he was murdered (probably on Gambino's orders) in 1957. Gambino took over and controlled the Mafia's New York operations, becoming a close associate of John Gotti. Gambino became ill in 1976 and appointed Paul Castellano as his successor, to ensure that there was no street battle for control of the family when he died.

See John Gotti p. 172

Carlo Gambino, 'The Godfather', is escorted by FBI agents in 1970.

Maranzano, Salvatore (1927–31)

Salvatore Maranzano came to America in 1927. He had been sent by the original Boss of Bosses in Sicily, Vito Cascio Ferro, who wanted him to bring the New York underworld under the control of the Sicilian mob.

Back in Italy, however, Ferro had been imprisoned by Mussolini's fascist government and this left Maranzano pretty much to his own devices, so he began to seek power for himself. Between 1928 and 1931, New York City and other crime capitals across the United States suffered the effects of the Castellemmarese War, in which Maranzano fought with the mobsters under the leadership of New York Mafia leader Joe 'The Boss' Masseria.

Maranzo's Murder

While the two factions fought, a younger and more power-hungry group arose under the command of Charlie 'Lucky' Luciano. On 10 September 1931, Luciano sent four of his own hand-picked hitmen, posing as IRS agents, to Maranzano's office. There, they stabbed and shot him to death. Along with Maranzano, 40 other associated figures in the crime world were murdered across the country. Luciano had been prompted to act when he learnt that Maranzano had called in Vincent 'Mad Dog' Coll to kill him.

See Lucky Luciano p. 169

Galante, Carmine (1940s-79)

Carmine Galante was born in 1910 and, after the death of Carlo Gambino in 1976, he made a play for the leadership of the Mafia. He had a rich pedigree in these circles, which began in the 1940s, and in 1978, had no fewer than eight major Mafia leaders killed to clear the road to succession. This, in addition to his major drug-trafficking activities, did not endear him to the other mob families, and on 12 July 1979, they had him killed.

Carmine Galante is carried from a Brooklyn restaurant after being shot in the eye.

Bonnano, Joseph (1960s)

Joseph Bonnano took control of his gang at the age of 26 – the youngest of all the crime-family dons. Under Bonnano's control, the family businesses prospered, and included interests in clothing and cheese factories, as well as funeral homes.

When Joseph Profaci, head of the Profaci family gang, died in 1962, Bonnano approached the new boss of the Profaci gang, Joe Maglicco, with a plan to kill Carlo Gambino, Thomas Luchese and Sam Giancana and take over their rackets. Maglicco passed the order to hitman Joe Colombo, but Colombo betrayed the plot.

Escape from La Cosa Nostra

La Cosa Nostra controlled the mafia families and settled disputes using the Commission, and so ordered Bonnano and Maglicco to appear before them and explain their actions. Bonnano refused and went into hiding. In 1964, Bonnano was kidnapped by his own enforcer Mike Zaffarano, and held for 19 months by his own cousin, Steven Magaddino. Bonnano agreed to retire and give up his family assets to the other members of La Cosa Nostra; he also agreed to live in exile in Haiti.

Bonnano Tells All

Bonnano was eventually allowed to return to America, provided he stay out of Mafia business. He lived in peace in Arizona with his family and some of his rackets that existed there. In 1983, he released his autobiography, which created a furore. When brought before a grand jury to answer questions regarding his book, he refused to respond. Bonnano died on 12 May 2002, at the age of 97.

Gotti, John (1960s–90s)

Gotti, born in 1940, was the head of the Gambino family of New York. Gotti had worked his way up in the family and in 1985, he arranged the shooting of his boss, Paul Castellano, in order to gain control. He became known as the 'Dapper Don' or the 'Teflon Don' because of his immaculate appearance and the fact that no charges against him ever seemed to stick.

Joseph Bonnano (Joe Bananas) arrives at the Federal Courthouse in New York, 1966.

Side-Stepping the Law

Gotti faced numerous charges over the years, but by using informants and intimidation he was able to stay one step ahead of the law. However, in April 1992 Gotti was convicted of 14 counts of murder, loan-sharking, racketeering, tax evasion, obstruction of justice (jury bribes and intimidation) and other crimes. This lengthy list led to a sentence of life imprisonment. He died in prison on 10 June 2002.

Castellano, Paul (1976-85)

Paul Castellano was born in Brooklyn in 1915. He was a member of the Gambino mobster family, and he married Carlo Gambino's sister. When Gambino died in 1976, he named Castellano his successor, with Aniello DelaCrosse as his second-in-command. Castellano ran the family like a regular business, even opening operations in Kuwait. When DelaCrosse died of lung cancer in December 1985, the other crime bosses decided it was time to kill Castellano and take control for themselves. On 16 December, Castellano and his driver were shot dead outside the Sparks Steak House in Manhattan.

See Carlo Gambino p. 170

Gravano, Salvatore (1970s-present)

Salvatore Gravano (Sammy 'The Bull') was under-boss to John Gotti, who was under-boss to the Gambino Mafia family. In 1990, Gravano turned against Gotti in an attempt to reduce the sentence he was likely to receive for his activities. He became the star witness against his old boss, receiving just five years, while Gotti was given life. Gravano then entered the Witness Protection Program.

Old Habits

Unable to stay away from a life of crime, Gravano was later arrested in Arizona as the head of an ecstasy trafficking ring. Now back in the public eye and of great interest to prosecutors, in 2003, he was charged with his involvement in a murder in 1980. He is currently in prison on drug charges.

Chicago Gangsters

The most famous of the Chicago gangsters, Al Capone, started his criminal career in New York, but moved to the Midwest to set up a syndicate there. Throughout the 1920s and 1930s, he and rival gangs fought deadly turf wars, the most famous result of which was the St Valentine's Day Massacre.

Capone, Al (1910s–1930s)

Al Capone was born in Brooklyn in 1899. He became involved with the Mafia at an early age, working for Johnny Torrio. He earned his nickname of 'Scarface' in 1917, after being slashed with a knife by Frank Galluccio, whose sister Capone had insulted. After a waterfront war with other gangs in 1918, Torrio decided to send Capone to Chicago. He arrived in 1920 and joined the Colosimo mob, which was mainly involved in illegal alcohol and similar rackets. Capone eventually killed Torrio's uncle, Colosimo, and took over the Chicago Mafia.

Gang Wars

Capone led Torrio's men against O'Banion's gang when the latter refused to accept Torrio as their boss. Torrio was nearly killed in the war and decided to retire and leave the business to Capone. By 1925, Capone could deploy 1,000 gunmen and, although he was a racketeer, murderer and bootlegger, his popularity was enormous. Rival gangs were extinguished – the most famous instance being the St Valentine's Day Massacre in 1929.

The Capture of Scarface

The US authorities had difficulty in finding any hard evidence against Capone for any of his illegal activities, but in 1931, they managed to take him to court on charges of tax evasion. He was

Notorious Mafia boss Al Capone smoking a cigar.

given a huge fine and a prison sentence. He was released in 1939 and he died of a stroke and pneumonia on 25 January 1947.

See St Valentine's Day Massacre p. 176

Torrio, Johnny (1910s–50s)

Torrio was born in Italy in 1882, but was raised in the ghettoes of New York. By 1912, he was involved in brothels, hijacking and extortion, and was working with a young Al Capone.

Battle with the O'Banions

Torrio had been working in Chicago for his uncle Big Jim Colosimo, dealing with anyone who tried to muscle in on the family business. Torrio eventually took over from Colosimo and united the Chicago gangs. Dion O'Banion, a Chicago gang leader, refused to be controlled by Torrio and was murdered. O'Banion's gang was taken over by Hymie Weiss and Bugs Moran, who vowed revenge.

On 24 January 1925, Weiss and Moran ambushed Torrio and badly wounded him; from then on, Torrio had 30 guards day and night. Torrio passed the business on to Capone, retiring as a millionaire to Brooklyn. Torrio died at the age of 75 in 1957.

Moran, George (1920s–40s)

George 'Bugs' Moran was born in 1893 and grew up in Chicago. He had served three prison terms by the time he was 21. He joined O'Banion's gang as a youth and took over leadership of the group in 1927 after his boss had been killed. As leader, he was involved in the turf war with Johnny Torrio and Al Capone and attempted to kill them; indeed, he had a pathological hatred of the man known as 'Scarface'. Moran was nearly killed in the St Valentine's Day Massacre, but was saved by arriving late at the meeting point. His gang was destroyed by Capone's attack, however, and he moved to Ohio where he was arrested in 1946 for robbing a bank messenger. He was given 10 years, but died of cancer in 1957 at the beginning of a second 10-year sentence for an earlier robbery. He was given a pauper's burial outside Leavenworth Prison.

St Valentine's Day Massacre (1929)

On 14 February 1929, Al Capone orchestrated one of the most famous Mafia hits of all time. Chicago North Side gang leader, Bugs Moran, refused to co-operate with Capone's image of a new Mafia order and Capone's plan was to put him permanently out of the picture.

The aftermath of the St Valentine's Day Massacre of 1929.

Murder in the Garage

Capone's assassination squad got into police uniforms and drove in a stolen police car over to the garage used by Moran's men. The bootleggers thought they had been caught in the act and lined up against a wall; the assassins then opened fire with two machine guns, a shotgun and a .45. The four assassins then left in the same car.

Consequences of the Massacre

Unfortunately, Moran was not one of the victims; he was late for the rendezvous with his gang. Capone had been popular with the public up to this point, but the massacre turned opinion against him; it also focused the attention of the law on Capone. He, as usual, had a cast-iron alibi; he was talking to a district attorney at the time!

See Al Capone p. 174

Nelson, Baby Face (1929-34)

Baby Face Nelson was born Lester Gillis in Chicago in 1908. He was only a petty criminal, but in 1929 that all changed when he began working for the notorious gang leader Al Capone. His youthful good looks earned him his nickname, which belied his willingness to carry out vicious killings. In 1934, he joined up with the John Dillinger gang, taking part in several bank robberies. He was killed in a shoot-out with the police and FBI on 27 November 1934.

Other American Gangsters

Organized crime in America has not, of course, been limited to Chicago and New York. Elsewhere in the USA, mobs carry out similar activities and engage in shady dealing. Sometimes, they manage to stay one step ahead of the law. Other times, they are not so lucky.

Dillinger, John (1924-34)

John Dillinger was born in Indianapolis in 1902. Even as a child, he was rebellious, joining the US Navy in 1923 but deserting a few months later. He committed his first robbery in September 1924, and was caught and imprisoned.

Bank Raids

While still on parole after his release in 1933, he began robbing banks in Indiana and Ohio. Dillinger was re-arrested, but his two partners, John Hamilton and Harry Pierpont, broke into the prison and released him. Between October 1933 and January 1934, the gang robbed a series of banks, netting over $100,000. They were arrested in Arizona, but Dillinger escaped in March and teamed up with Baby Face Nelson to commit more bank robberies. Dillinger was finally killed in a police ambush in Chicago on 22 July 1934.

John Dillinger travels under heavy escort to Indiana. charged with murdering a policeman.

Hoffa, Jimmy (1933-75)

Jimmy Hoffa was born in 1913 and rose to become a major American labour leader with Mafia connections. Hoffa's union activities began in 1933 and he proved to be a natural leader. He rapidly rose in the ranks of the Teamsters Union (truck drivers), taking over from the jailed Dave Beck in the 1950s. He co-operated with the Mafia to control entire industries in America and allowed the theft of money from the Teamsters Union pension funds to be used by the Mafia.

The Mystery of Hoffa's Fate

In 1967, he was convicted of attempted bribery of a jury and given 15 years. His associates funded Richard Nixon's presidential campaign and Hoffa was released in 1971. Hoffa mysteriously disappeared on 31 July 1975. His body was never found and he was pronounced dead in 1981.

Jimmy Hoffa, president of the Teamsters Union, at a 1959 press conference.

See The Mafia p. 164

Bulger, James J. (1960s-present)

James 'Whitey' Bulger has been described by the FBI as a major figure in the world of organized crime in the Boston area. He is currently one of the FBI's Ten Most Wanted and is being sought for extortion and racketeering influenced and corruption organization (RICO) charges.

Most Wanted

Over the years, Bulger has funded his activities through criminal operations in Boston. His business interests include gambling, loan-sharking and drugs. Bulger is well travelled in Italy, Ireland and Canada. The alleged don of the Winter Hill Gang in South Boston, Bulger is known to have a violent temper and usually carries a knife. He was indicted in October 2000 for his involvement in 19 murders in the Boston area. There is a reward of $1 million for information leading to his arrest.

See The Mafia p. 164

FBI TEN MOST WANTED FUGITIVE

RACKETEERING INFLUENCED AND CORRUPT ORGANIZATIONS (RICO) - MURDER (18 COUNTS), CONSPIRACY TO COMMIT MURDER, CONSPIRACY TO COMMIT EXTORTION, NARCOTICS DISTRIBUTION, CONSPIRACY TO COMMIT MONEY LAUNDERING; EXTORTION; MONEY LAUNDERING

JAMES J. BULGER

Photograph taken in 1994   Photograph taken in 1994   Photograph altered in 2000

An FBI Ten Most Wanted poster of James J Bulger.

Murphy, Sandy and Tabish, Rick (1998-present)

Murphy was convicted of the 1998 killing of multi-millionaire gaming executive Ted Binion. Binion was an associate of mobster Herbert 'Fat Herbie' Blitzstein, who was found shot dead in his Las Vegas home on 7 January 1997, the victim of an organized crime killing. Also convicted on a first-degree murder charge was Murphy's lover, Rick Tabish. Authorities said the pair either forced Binion to ingest a lethal amount of drugs or suffocated him; they were sentenced to life with a possibility of parole after 20 years. On 14 July 2003, however, the US Supreme Court overturned the convictions, saying the pair's 2000 trial was flawed. They were granted a retrial and acquitted of murder but convicted on lesser charges. Tabish was released in 2010.

See The Mafia p. 164

British Gangsters

London was naturally the heart of gangland in Britain. Here, racketeers such as the infamous Kray twins plied their trade throughout the 1950s and 1960s. Other forms of organized crime reared their heads in this period – the bestknown of which was the Great Train Robbery.

Fraser, Mad Frankie (1930s-90s)

Fraser was born in 1923 and his criminal career spanned the period of the Sabini gang and the Kray twins in London. Fraser won his nickname after a violent attack on Jack Spot in Praed Street, Paddington, on 2 May 1956. From 1936, Fraser spent 32 of the next 40 years in prison for a variety of criminal offences; indeed, he spent a total of 40 years at Her Majesty's pleasure. He had a reputation as one of the Richardson gang's torturers and allegedly pulled out teeth with pliers. Fraser was shot in the head outside a nightclub in Farringdon in August 1991, but he survived and has written books on his exploits; he also conducts gangland tours around London. Two home secretaries labelled Fraser 'the most dangerous man in Britain'.

Ronald and Reginald Kray at aged 18.

The Kray Twins (1950s-69)

Twins Ronnie and Reggie Kray had been in trouble with the law since their mid-teens, when they were charged with gangland violence in Hackney, London. By the 1950s, they had set up protection rackets and in 1960, opened a gambling club in the West End.

Rising Notoriety

In the mid to late 1960s, they began to hit the headlines. Ronnie shot George Cornell in the Blind Beggar pub in the East End on 9 March 1966, after Cornell had called him 'a fat poof'; Cornell was a principle member of the gang led by Charlie and Eddie Richardson. In November, Reggie stabbed Jack 'The Hat' McVitie to death in a flat in Stoke Newington; later, they would also be linked with the murder of Frank 'Mad Axeman' Mitchell in December.

The Fate of the Krays

In 1969, the twins were sentenced to 30 years, along with their elder brother, Charlie, who was given seven years. They became the longest-serving prisoners in recent British history – Ronnie died in prison in 1995. In 1998, Reggie's parole application was refused; he also died in prison in 2000, after serving 31 years. Their brother Charlie also died in 2000, whilst serving a prison sentence for having masterminded a £69 million cocaine-smuggling plot.

Richardson, Charlie and Eddie (1960s)

The infamous Kray twins, Ronnie and Reggie, shared control of London with the Richardson gang, which was based in South London. The gang consisted of brothers Charlie and Eddie Richardson, Mad Frankie Fraser and George Cornell. Their primary business was fraud, but in the 1960s, they began supplying West End clubs with gambling machines. By 1965, the gang had effectively been put out of business by the police and the brothers were briefly imprisoned. In March 1966, they were involved in a gun battle with the Krays, during which Fraser and Eddie were both shot. Later

London gangland boss Charlie Richardson at the funeral of the infamous gangster Lenny Maclean.

that year, Cornell was murdered by the Krays and the Richardson brothers began a 25-year prison sentence for fraud-related crimes.

See Mad Frankie Fraser p. 180

The Great Train Robbery (1963)

The Great Train Robbery took place on 8 August 1963 at Cheddington, Buckinghamshire, when a Royal Mail train was stopped near a bridge by a criminal gang who had tampered with the signals. The gang was led by Bruce Reynolds and included Ronnie Biggs, Buster Edwards, Brian Field, Gordon Goody, Charlie Wilson, Jimmy Hussey, John Wheater, Jimmy White, Tommy Wisbey and five others. The only injury during the robbery was suffered by the train driver, Jack Mills, who was struck with an iron bar. He never fully recovered and died in 1970. Royal Mail staff put up no resistance and the gang got away with £2.6 million.

Post Office and railway workers unload the remaining bags following the Great Train Robbery.

The Flight of the Robbers

The police found their Oxfordshire hideout covered in fingerprints, and managed to round up the culprits. They were tried and sentenced to a total of 307 years. Edwards gave himself up after fleeing to Mexico for three years. After 15 months in prison, Biggs and Reynolds escaped; Biggs settled in Brazil. Reynolds was on the run for five years in Mexico and Canada after the 1963 robbery, until his £150,000 share ran out and he was eventually caught, penniless, in Torquay. Wilson escaped in 1964 and was on the run for four years, but was recaptured in 1968. The lost money has never been recovered.

Biggs, Ronald (1963)

Ronald Biggs, the public face of Britain's Great Train Robbery, actually played a fairly minor part in the crime. After being sentenced to 25 years, he spent just 15 months in Wandsworth Prison before escaping and fleeing Britain. He had plastic surgery to change his appearance and moved to Spain, then Australia and finally Brazil. Biggs remained there for many years and made a good living from his fame. Illness finally forced him back to Britain in May 2001 and despite his age (71) and ill-health, he was sent back to prison to serve out his sentence. He was controversially released from prison in August 2009 on compassionate grounds.

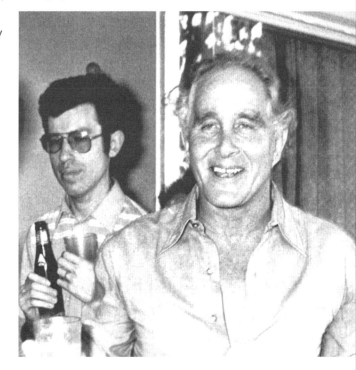

Great Train Robber Ronnie Biggs celebrates after being freed by the Supreme Court in 1981.

8

Getting Away With Murder?

There are many instances where miscarriages of justice have come to light – when the wrong person has been accused and punished. But there are also many cases where people have been acquitted, despite compelling evidence of their guilt. Have these people really got away with murder?

The Odd Case of Edmund Pook (1871)

In 1871, epileptic Edmund Pook from Greenwich began a relationship with the household domestic servant, Jane Clouson. When she was violently murdered on 26 April, she was found to be two months pregnant. Bloodstains were discovered on Edmund's coat and he was identified as having purchased a hammer, believed to be the murder weapon. Despite all this, Edmund was found not guilty.

See The Bootlace Murders p. 216

A newspaper artist's impression of the Edmund Pook case.

The Murder of Georgina Moore (1882)

In 1882, the court and newspapers were more interested in Stephen Moore's love life than who killed his eight-year-old daughter, Georgina. Her body had been found near the home of one of Stephen's former lovers – Esther Pay – in Yarnley, Kent. She was suspected of having killed Georgina in revenge for being abandoned by him. The jury believed she had no motive and cleared her.

See Jeannie Ewan Donald p. 127

The Providence House Murder (1901)

On the morning of 1 June 1901, the body of Rose Harsent was discovered by her father in the kitchen of Providence House in Peasenhall, Suffolk. Someone had tried, unsuccessfully, to burn the body. Her throat had been cut twice and there was a wound in her chest.

The Suspect

Suspicion immediately fell upon William Gardiner, who had been having an affair with Rose for several months. It was the gossip of the village that this Methodist elder, with a pregnant wife and children of his own, had been sleeping with Rose. When it was discovered at the inquest that Rose was heavily pregnant and that she and Gardiner had exchanged notes, it was inevitable that Gardiner would face a trial for her murder.

Trial and Acquittal

The evidence was circumstantial, but the trial took place at the beginning of November 1902. After considerable deliberation, the jury told the court that they were unable to agree a verdict. It was therefore decided that Gardiner should face trial once more. This began in January 1903; the same evidence was brought forward, laced with gossip, scandal and innuendo. Again, the jury was unable to agree. Gardiner was cleared. It has been speculated that the real murderer was his wife, Georgina.

See Alice Crimmins p. 197

The Camden Town Murder (1907)

On 12 September 1907, the body of Camden Town prostitute Emily Dimmock was found by the man with whom she shared a home, Bertram Shaw. Meanwhile, another prostitute, Ruby Young,

Artist Robert Wood, who was arrested and tried for the murder of a prostitute.

had been asked by her artist lover, Robert Wood, to provide him with an alibi. She told a friend of Wood's request, who in turn contacted the police. Wood eventually faced trial, although the evidence was circumstantial, but he was found not guilty.

The Sacco and Vanzetti Case (1920)

On 15 April 1920, in South Braintree, Massachusetts, a robbery led to a double murder. Quite by accident, two Italians, Sacco and Vanzetti, were questioned, as they had a similar vehicle to that used in the robbery. In a highly racist trial, the pair were found guilty of robbery and murder and sentenced to death; they were electrocuted on 23 August 1927. In 1977, their names were cleared by the governor of Massachusetts.

Crowds stage a demonstration to free Sacco and Vanzetti.

See The Lindbergh Case p. 202

The Hoop-La Murder (1933)

The trial of Jessie Costello for the murder of her husband – using potassium cyanide, a compound used to burnish kitchen boilers – was described as one of the most astonishing crime farces in American criminal history.

Profit from the Crime

From the moment she was arrested on 17 March 1933, Costello became the darling of the press and the public for her undoubted sex appeal. There was never any chance that she would be found guilty and indeed, she was acquitted. But for some time, America could not forget her and she made a good living selling her story and posing for photographs.

Nonetheless, just 12 months after her acquittal, she had run out of money and lived the rest of her life on $65 a month from state aid.

See Adelaide Bartlett p. 221

The Black Dahlia (1947)

The naked body of Elizabeth Short was found on waste land near Los Angeles on 15 January 1947; her body had virtually been cut in half at the waist and the letters 'BD' had been carved into her thigh. Short, an aspiring film star, had been known as the Black Dahlia. Like many hopefuls, she had been disillusioned by Hollywood and had slipped into prostitution and alcoholism.

Dead End in the Dahlia Case

There were several false confessions, but no real leads, until a note arrived at a Los Angeles newspaper office, along with a package containing Short's birth certificate, address book and social security card. The note promised that Short's clothes would be sent in another parcel. The

Robert Manley is given a lie detector test over the murder of Elizabeth Short in 1947.

FBI thoroughly checked the documents for fingerprints, but none matched any on their files. The most promising lead they had was an unnamed army corporal, who told them, 'When I get drunk, I get rough with women'. His background and movements were checked, but he was released as the police believed him to be mentally unbalanced. Theories and suspects abounded in the following years, but the murderer of the Black Dahlia was never found.

The Suzy Lamplugh Case (1986)

Missing estate agent Suzy Lamplugh, who vanished in July 1986.

Estate agent Suzy Lamplugh disappeared while meeting an unknown client called Mr Kipper in Fulham, south-west London, in 1986. Her body has never been found. Police are currently studying claims that her remains may be buried at the former house of the mother of the man who is suspected of the murder – a convicted rapist and murderer called John Cannan who is serving life for the killing of Bristol woman Shirley Banks.

The Wrong Man?

In December 2002, newspaper reports claimed that in letters written by Cannan, he mentioned that he had blood stains on his coat when laying a patio at his mother's home in Solihull a year after Suzy went missing. In January 2003, Cannan went to the High Court to secure 'free and unimpeded' access to his legal advisors. He claimed the governor of the maximum-security prison in Yorkshire where he is serving his sentence has violated his human rights, by preventing him from exchanging legal documents with his solicitors. His case was dismissed, but he may appeal.

The Rachel Nickell Case (1992)

On 13 July 1992 the body of Rachel Nickell was found on Wimbledon Common. She had been stabbed 49 times in just three minutes, in full sight of her two-year-old son. The police released a psychological profile of the man who may have perpetrated the crime, and were approached by a woman called Julie Pine, who had received letters from her pen-friend, a man called Colin Stagg. She and the police both thought there was a connection between Stagg and the killing.

Hunting Stagg

The police used an undercover agent calling herself Lizzie James and, over the course of five months, she attempted to obtain a confession from him. It was a classic example of entrapment; Stagg and Lizzie met a total of four times and they discussed Rachel's murder, which Stagg described incorrectly. Nonetheless, the police amassed 700 pages of transcripts and intended to take Stagg to court. A judge ruled that the evidence was inadmissible and that the undercover operation had proved nothing. However, Stagg's name has been for ever linked to the Nickell murder and the police have never been able to establish who really carried out the killing on Wimbledon Common.

Simpson, O.J. (1994)

Orenthal James Simpson was one of the most famous running-backs in American football history. He retired from the game in 1979 and married Nicole Brown, his second wife, in 1985. It was a rocky marriage and Nicole filed for divorce in 1992. There had been incidents in the marriage that suggested that Simpson may have been a violent man.

The Events Unfold

On 12 June 1994, Nicole and a restaurant employee, Ronald Goldman, were found brutally murdered and five days later millions of television viewers watched a long, slow police chase that finally ended with the arrest of a suicidal Simpson. Although he claimed to be innocent, he was charged with the murder of Nicole and Goldman. The year-long trial was televised, with the witnesses and court officials becoming household names in what was dubbed the 'Trial of the Century'.

Simpson's Acquittal

On 4 October 1995, Simpson was acquitted, but in the following civil trial, he was found liable for the deaths of Brown and Goldman. In February 1997, the jury ordered Simpson to pay $33.5 million in compensatory and punitive damages. Evidence is slowly emerging about Goldman's ties to organized crime and a Colombian drug cartel.

Sinister Practices

The unsavoury practices indulged in by some criminals have often given investigators pause for thought, and the horrific ways in which some murderers have killed their victims, or attempted to dispose of the bodies, remain burned in the public memory.

Burke, William and Hare, William (1828)

William Burke and William Hare were Irish labourers living in West Port, one of the slum areas of Edinburgh. When one of the lodgers in their rooms died owing rent, they hit upon the idea of selling her body to a Dr Knox, who was always interested in obtaining bodies for dissection. Amazed at the price they received, they set about providing corpses for the doctor by the simple expedient of murdering vagrants and beggars. Over the next nine months, they delivered 16 bodies to Knox.

The police eventually linked them to the disappearances and charged them. Hare testified against Burke and their accomplice, Nell MacDougal, received a 'not proven' verdict. Burke was hanged at Edinburgh's Grass Market on 28 January 1829. His body was sent for dissection.

See Issei Sagawa p. 194

William Burke, a murderer and body snatcher who was hanged for his crimes, and his accomplice William Hare.

WILLIAM BURKE.
THE MURDERER

WILLIAM HARE.
KING'S EVIDENCE

Haigh, John George (1949)

In 1949, John George Haigh, who was known to be something of a charmer, became friendly with a wealthy widow named Olive Durand-Deacon. They talked about starting a business together. On 18 February 1949, he took her to Crawley in Sussex to visit his factory. Haigh had made preparations; he had bought an empty 40-gallon drum, rubber gloves and an apron and a considerable quantity of sulphuric acid. Once inside, he shot the widow, took her valuables and then put her into the drum, which he then filled with the sulphuric acid.

Capture of the Acid Bath Killer

Shortly afterwards, he reported the widow's disappearance to the police. They checked their records and discovered that Haigh had a criminal

'Acid bath' murderer John George Haigh during his 1949 trial.

record, so visited the Crawley factory. Fragments of the widow were found, along with a revolver and traces of blood. Haigh was arrested, but told the police that they could not prove anything without a body; he also admitted to eight other murders, believing that he had disposed of the evidence. Police found an acrylic denture belonging to the widow in the sludge at the bottom of the barrel and Haigh faced a murder trial in July 1949. He claimed that he was insane and that he had drunk his victims' blood. He was found guilty and executed on 10 August 1949.

See Harvey Hawley Crippen p. 201

Staniak, Lucian (1964-67)

Lucian Staniak, a Polish serial killer operating between July 1964 and January 1967, was known as the 'Red Spider' because he sent anonymous letters to either newspapers or the police, warning them that he was going to commit murder, written in spidery, red handwriting. His victims were young women who he either strangled or stabbed; after death, he raped them, then mutilated their bodies. After investigation, Warsaw police realized the murderer was travelling to the scenes by train.

Trapping the Red Spider

The arty writing and red paint used suggested an artist, which led the police to Staniak; they found knives and red art paint in his locker. Staniak confessed to 20 murders and was sentenced to death for the six known killings. His sentence was commuted to life and he was sent to an asylum.

See Nikolai Dzhumagaliev p. 68

Chase, Richard Trenton (1977)

Richard Trenton Chase, who became known as the 'Sacramento Vampire', began by killing animals and drinking their blood, eating birds alive and injecting himself with rabbit blood. His schizophrenia saw him in and out of mental institutions until 1976, but in January 1977, he went on a four-day murder spree, killing six people and drinking their blood. After the killings, he took various parts of their bodies with him to gnaw on later. On 26 December 1980, Chase was found dead in his prison cell; he had committed suicide by hoarding three weeks' worth of medication and taking it all in one dose.

See Marc Sappington p. 196

Sagawa, Issei (1981)

In 1981, Issei Sagawa, Japanese by birth, was studying in Paris. Obsessed with tall, blonde women, he focused on one such, Renée Hartvelt, shooting her on 11 June 1981. He claimed he had always wished to show a woman his love by eating her; this he did to Renée. Two days later, he was arrested and confessed. After transfer to Japan, he was freed in 1985 and has been featured on the front of a Japanese gourmet magazine.

Issei Sagawa arrives in Tokyo accused of murdering and consuming parts of a woman.

Clark, Hadden (1992)

In 1992, Hadden Clark was arrested for the murder of 23-year-old Laurie Houghteling in Bethesda, Maryland. Clark was a transvestite and a cannibal, believing that by killing and eating women, he would become one himself. Clark would later admit to the murder of at least 12 women, including a six-year-old girl, Michele Dorr. His first trial in Maryland gained him 30 years imprisonment; a second, in 1999, a full life sentence. Clark continues to make prison confessions to a fellow inmate, who he believes to be Jesus, and has often taken the police to try to find the shallow graves of his victims. Each time, he is dressed as a woman and is known as Kristen.

The Snowtown Murders (1994–97)

The residents of the small South Australian town of Snowtown never suspected that in the old bank just across the road from the pub was a terrible secret – six barrels full of human remains. There were 10 victims, allegedly killed for little more than their pension money.

A Gruesome Discovery

Police who broke into the locked bank vault found putrid human remains, handcuffs and an electric-shock machine. The victims had been either strangled or asphyxiated. Several of them were found with gags stuffed in their mouths, others had ropes around their necks; feet and limbs had been amputated and there were burns on some of the bodies. The killings were allegedly carried out as part of a macabre social-security fraud.

The Murderers on Trial

John Justin Bunting, Mark Ray Haydon, James Vlassakis and Robert Joe Wagner were charged with between four and 10 of the murders. Bunting, Haydon and Wagner were also charged with the murder of Thomas Trevilyan, whose body was found hanging from a tree in Adelaide in 1997. In addition, Haydon and Bunting were also charged with the murder of Clinton Trezise, who was found in a shallow grave at Lower Light, north of Adelaide, in 1994. Committal proceedings continue.

Sappington, Marc (2001)

In March 2001, Marc Sappington became a murderer by shooting David Mashak in an aggravated robbery at a car dealership. In April the same year, Sappington answered the voices in his head, which were telling him to harvest human flesh and blood. In accordance with the voices' orders, he began his killing spree. He killed three people, two in one day; all were known to him. Sappington was dubbed the 'Kansas City Vampire' after it emerged he drank his victims' blood; it is also alleged that he ate part of the leg of one of them.

Intense Manhunt

Sappington's mother discovered a body in her basement and called the police, who soon tracked down Sappington. He jumped into a car, however, and led police on a brief chase. After his arrest he was held in a state hospital and underwent a series of psychological tests where it was concluded that he severely mentally ill. In 2004 he was deemed fit to stand trial, and was given four consecutive life sentences. Sappington will spend the rest of his life in an asylum.

Child Murders

How anyone can kill a child is beyond the imagination of most people. From instances where someone takes the life of their own child, to serial child killers such as Fred and Rosemary West, these are the cases that truly cause national mourning and outrage.

Crimmins, Alice (1965)

Alice Crimmins, charged with murder, outside the New York courthouse in 1968.

On 14 July 1965, Alice Marie and Eddie Crimmins' father reported his children missing. They were living in New York with their mother, Alice. Later that day, Alice Marie's body was found and a few days later, Eddie's body was also discovered; they had both been strangled. Nearly two years after the murders, Alice was charged with her daughter's killing and a witness testified at her May 1968 trial that she had been seen with a man carrying a bundle and holding her daughter in her arms. She was found guilty of manslaughter and sentenced to 20 years. In March 1971, Alice was charged with the murder of her son; again, she was found guilty and sentenced to life. The apparent motive was that she feared their father would win a custody battle.

See Susan Barber p. 131

Henley, Elmer Wayne and Brooks, David (1973)

In the period leading up to 8 August 1973, Elmer Wayne Henley and David Brooks lured 27 boys to the home of Dean Allen Corll, for which they were paid $200 per boy.

The Suppliers Turn

At Corll's house, the boys were drugged, subjected to sexual assaults and mutilated until finally they were either strangled or shot. On 8 August, Henley brought a girl to Corll, who turned on his suppliers. Henley drugged them all and tied them to a rack and told Corll that he would not be killed if he raped then shot the girl. Corll did not and so Henley shot him six times. He then called the police and showed them where the 27 bodies had been hidden.

In July 1974, he and Brooks were sentenced to six consecutive 99-year jail terms for Corll's murder and their involvement in the killing of the boys.

See Fred and Rosemary West p. 87

Police recover a body from the rented boat shed where Elmer Henley led them.

Jones, Genene (1981)

Between May and December 1981, the paediatric department at the Bexar County Hospital in San Antonio, Texas, saw the deaths of 20 infants. A drug called heparin, a blood-thinning agent, was discovered in one of the victims' bodies. There were a number of internal enquiries and one nurse accused Genene Jones of having killed the children. Speculation linked her to as many as 42 deaths. Jones was sentenced to 99 years on specimen charges.

Allitt, Beverly (1991)

Allitt suffered from Munchausen's syndrome by proxy, a disorder that creates an uncontrollable urge to draw attention, and in Allitt's case by causing injury to babies in her care. A career as a nurse provided her with that very opportunity. In February 1991, Beverly Allitt began a new job as staff nurse in the children's ward at the Grantham and Kesteven Hospital in Lincolnshire.

The Angel of Death

Allitt's first victim died of heart failure on 21 February. No-one suspected at that point that she'd had any part in this baby's tragic death as she was so attentive and reassuring to the baby's parents. Over the next 58 days she killed three more children and injured a further nine. During this period, medical staff did not realise there was a killer in their midst, although there were many suspicious episodes. Alarm bells finally rang in late April after yet another baby

Child–killer Beverly Allitt arrives at court in 1991.

died following a cardiac arrest. The staff could no longer hide from the fact that something was terribly wrong on the ward. The police were called in and investigations began.

Painstaking Enquiry

When the enquiry began, it was found that a number of the bodies contained high potassium levels, others showed high levels of insulin, substances which can induce cardiac arrest and lethal hypoglycemia. Staff rotas for the period in question were checked, and Allitt was the only nurse to have been on duty during every suspicious episode. On 22 April 1991 she was formally charged, but did not stand trial until 15 February 1993. The jury found her guilty of murder and attempted murder on 11 May 1993 and she was given 13 life sentences.

Pandy, Andras (1997)

On 20 October 1997, Belgian authorities charged Andras Pandy with the murder of two of his ex-wives and four of his children. Large pieces of human flesh had been found in his fridges and he may have been responsible for as many as 14 killings.

Police Hunt

Pandy, Hungarian by birth, had moved to Belgium in 1957 and was a former Protestant pastor. In a joint operation between Belgian and Hungarian police, following child-abuse accusations against Pandy, his two homes were searched. A series of interconnecting cellars were found in the homes where Pandy and his daughter Agnes carried out the murders and the disposal of the corpses.

Remaining Questions

Belgian police believe that the Pandy in custody may actually be the younger brother of the real Andras Pandy, who may have died in 1956. Pandy is also believed to have adopted an unspecified number of Romanian orphans who are also missing. On 8 March 2002, a jury convicted Pandy of six counts of murder. He was also convicted of raping his daughters. Agnes Pandy was convicted of five counts of murder and of the attempted murder of her stepsister Timea. Agnes Pandy was sentenced to 21 years in prison.

Other Investigations

Some cases are so intriguing they are bound to make headline news. The wrong suspect ... a copycat killer ... a doctor of death ... and the most famous kidnapping of all time, the mystery of which still has not been fully explained.

The Railway Murder (1905)

In September 1905, a railway inspector discovered the grisly remains of a woman who had been bound and gagged, then thrown out of a train into Merstham Tunnel in London. The body was identified by Robert Money, who confirmed it was his sister, Mary. Despite investigation, the police could not find the murderer and the case remained unsolved.

Unravelling the Mystery

On 18 August 1911, police were called to a house in Eastbourne that had been gutted by fire. Inside, they found the bodies of one Robert Murray, also known as Mackie, and the children of Florence, who had herself survived a gunshot and managed to get out of the house. It transpired that Murray and Money were the same person, and that whilst he was living with Florence as her husband, he had in fact married Florence's sister, Edith, in secret. His suicide note was found, so Florence had presumably discovered his bigamy and he had set fire to the house.

See The Camden Town Murder p. 187

Crippen, Harvey Hawley (1910)

In 1900, Michigan-born Dr Hawley Harvey Crippen came to England. Crippen worked for a patent medicine company and moved into a home with his new wife, actress Cora Turner, whose stage name was Belle Elmore. Belle disappeared in 1910 and Crippen told everyone that she had returned to the US.

Suspicions are Roused

However, Belle's friends noticed that Ethel le Neve, who soon moved in with Crippen, was wearing the missing woman's clothes. The police began an investigation, but found nothing. Police interest obviously alarmed Crippen, though, and he fled to Antwerp with le Neve. There, the couple boarded the SS Montrose, bound for Canada. Crippen's flight rekindled police interest and they went to his old house, where they found Belle's body in the cellar.

THE WESTERN UNION TELEGRAPH COMPANY.

Wireless Saves the Day

Le Neve had disguised herself as a boy for the voyage to Canada, but the ship's captain was suspicious of the fact that the couple were openly affectionate. He radioed London – the first time the wireless was used as part of a murder hunt. Chief Inspector Walter Dew boarded a faster ship and was awaiting Crippen when they docked. Crippen and le Neve were sent back to Britain; he was found guilty of murder and hanged on 23 November 1910.

See John George Haigh p. 193

The Crippen case marked the first use of wireless telegraphy in the arrest of criminals.

The Lindbergh Case (1932)

On 1 March 1932, the baby son of pioneer aviator Charles Lindbergh was kidnapped from his home in Hopewell, New Jersey. Over the next few weeks, intricate arrangements were made to pay $50,000 in notes and $20,000 in gold bonds as a ransom. The police had no real clues to the kidnapper's identity; all they knew was that he had a German accent. The ransom was paid, but it turned out that the child had already been murdered.

Who Was the Real Lindbergh Kidnapper?

The kidnapper laid low for three years, and in an effort to draw him out, police asked the banks to announce that gold bonds were about to be withdrawn and that they should be cashed immediately. Bruno Hauptmann was apprehended while attempting to cash one of the bonds at a garage in New Jersey. He claimed from the outset that he was merely looking after the money for a friend who had recently died in Germany. The only other evidence linking Hauptmann to the crime was that the wood in his attic matched that which had been used to make a ladder to reach the boy's bedroom. Hauptmann was sent to the electric chair in 1935, still protesting his innocence.

The clothes worn by Charles Lindbergh Jr at the time of his kidnapping are shown in court.

Hanratty, James (1961)

On the evening of 22 August 1961, lovers Michael Gregsten and Valerie Storie were parked in a field near Slough, Buckinghamshire. They were approached by a man with a gun and told to drive to a lay-by on the A6. The gunman shot Gregsten and raped Storie, then shot her and made off in the car. Incredibly, Storie survived and, together with another witness who had seen Gregsten's car after the murder, two identikit pictures were created; neither resembled Hanratty, but two cartridge cases were found at a London hotel in a room that he had occupied. Hanratty was arrested and claimed he had been in Rhyl on the day of the murder. The jury was unconvinced and found him guilty; he was hanged on 4 April 1962.

This is my son. JAMES HANRATT murdered by the sta for the A.6. mu

ELEVEN WITNESSES SWEAR H WAS IN RHYL. 200 MILES AWA

The father of alleged A6 killer James Hanratty protests his son's innocence in 1970.

Harvey, Donald (1983-86)

Between April 1983 and September 1986, Donald Harvey, the self-professed 'Angel of Death', committed innumerable murders of patients at the Drake Memorial Hospital in Cincinnati, Ohio. On 11 August 1987, after extensive enquiries and a mountain of evidence, including poisons and a diary, Harvey admitted to 33 murders over the previous 17 years. Ultimately, he confessed to 70. On 18 August, he pleaded guilty to 24 counts of murder, four of attempted murder and one count of assault. He was given four life sentences. In Kentucky in September, he was given a further eight life sentences for 12 murders and in February 1988, three life sentences for three murders and three attempted murders. Harvey's first scheduled parole hearing is in 2047, by which time he will be 95.

The Hilda Murrell Case (1984)

On 24 March 1984, the half-naked body of Hilda Murrell was found in a copse near Shrewsbury. The probable cause of death was hypothermia. As the police investigated who was responsible for her death, they found evidence that linked Murrell with the nuclear power industry and British intelligence. She had confided to friends that she thought she was under surveillance. It appears that MI5 had used freelance operatives to search Murrell's home, believing she was on the verge of exposing serious deficiencies in the nuclear reactors at Sizewell. Unsubstantiated evidence suggests that Murrell had caught them in the act, and that they had panicked and killed her. It is possible that the killer was a man variously known as Vic Norris and Adrian Hampson, a convicted child abuser.

See The Sacco and Vanzetti Case p. 188

Hilda Murrell – undercover operative?

Seda, Heriberto (1990)

An uncaught serial killer terrorized the Bay Area in the 1960s and 1970s, but a bizarre and cryptic letter arrived at East New York's 17th Precinct on 17 November 1989, claiming to be from the Zodiac killer himself, predicting a new wave of murders.

Signs of the Zodiac

In March 1990, the killings began, just as the letter had predicted, and it soon became clear that the police were dealing with a copycat murderer. The killer was Heriberto 'Eddie' Seda and he revelled in the press coverage he was receiving. After a siege, he turned himself over to the police and in June 1998, he was sentenced to 236 years. His tally was three dead and eight attempted murders.

See The Zodiac Killer p. 212

9

Serial Killings

Jack the Ripper... the Zodiac Killer... the Cleveland Torso Killer... These names have gone down in legend, and they have done so because their true identities remain a mystery. These are the most notorious serial killers of all time – simply because they were never caught.

Jack the Ripper (1888)

In the autumn of 1888, the most notorious murderer in British history stalked the East End streets of London, mutilating and then killing at least five prostitutes. The savage attacks, increasing in ferocity over the few short weeks, terrorized London and the police seemed unable to find a credible suspect or protect the street women.

The Ripper's Victims

Mary Ann Nicholls (43) was the first acknowledged victim; she was lashed across the throat and repeatedly stabbed on 31 August . Annie Chapman (47) had many of her organs removed on 8 September; the attack on Elizabeth Stride (45) may have been interrupted on 30 September, but the same night, the Ripper mutilated Catherine Eddowes (46). The last and most vicious dismemberment took place on 9 November, when the Ripper claimed his last victim, Mary Kelly (25).

Cover of the *Penny Illustrated Paper* showing one of Jack the Ripper's victims.

What Happened to the Ripper?

During the killing spree, the police and newspapers were taunted with letters purporting to have been written by the Ripper. One even contained Eddowes' kidney, part of which the Ripper claimed to have fried and eaten. The police were inundated with theories and potential suspects but, as suddenly as the killings had begun, they abruptly ended. Writers still speculate as to the identity of the Ripper.

See The Zodiac Killer p. 212

The Axe-Man of New Orleans (1911–19)

Between 1911 and 1919, there was a series of violent murders; it appeared that robbery was not the motive and the weapon used was often the property of the victim. What was particularly bizarre in the case of these killings was the accusations of some of the victims who survived.

The Wrong Man?

On 28 June 1918, Louis Besumer and Harriet Lowe were attacked by the axe-man; Lowe was killed but before she died, she denounced Besumer. On 10 March 1919, however, the axe-man struck again, injuring Charles and Rosie Cortimiglia and killing Mary, their daughter. Rosie denounced her neighbours, one of whom was sentenced to death and the other given life imprisonment. But the axe-man struck again in September and October. The last victim's wife shot Joseph Mumfre, claiming he was the axe-man. There were no more murders but also no proof against Mumfre.

See The Moonlight Murders p. 224

The Cleveland Torso Killer (1935–38)

In September 1935, the heavily mutilated bodies of two decapitated men were discovered, and police initially suspected that they were dealing with a homosexual killer. However, the next two bodies they found were female. Over the next three years, 12 victims were claimed. The famous detective Elliot Ness was brought in to lead investigations and in August 1938, he rounded up vagrants and burned down the area where the bodies had been found; the murders stopped. His suspects were Frank Dolezal and a man known as Sundheim, but in April 1939, Dolezal committed suicide. Sundheim was committed to a mental institution, where he died; no clear link was established.

Jack the Stripper (1964-65)

A string of six near-identical killings, known as the Hammersmith Nudes Case, occurred between February 1964 and February 1965. They were the first modern UK crimes to be recognized as serial killings.

Copycat Killer

The naked bodies of six prostitutes – Hannah Tailford, Irene Lockwood, Helen Barthelemey, Mary Fleming, Margaret McGowan and Bridie O'Hara – were found in and around the Hammersmith area. Most of the women had severe bruising to the jaw and their front teeth were missing. It later transpired that the women had been forced to strip and then engage in violent oral sex.

The Investigation

There was a breakthrough of sorts when it was established that the women had all been abducted between 11 p.m. and 1 a.m. and that their bodies had been dumped between 5 a.m. and 6 a.m. The focus of investigations switched to night-shift workers. Microscopic flakes of paint were found on Barthelemey's and Fleming's bodies, narrowing the search to car-spraying workers. All businesses nearby were inspected and a list of suspects drawn up, but no arrest or charge was ever made. In the investigating officer's memoirs, a 45-year-old night security guard was identified as Jack the Stripper; he committed suicide during the investigation of the case.

See Jack the Ripper p. 208

The Monster of Florence (1968-85)

The mystery of the 'Monster of Florence' began in August 1968 with the murder of Barbara Locci, a 32-year-old married woman, and her lover Antonio Lo Bianco. The police interviewed

Stefano Mele, Barbara's husband; he listed all her lovers, including Francesco Vinci and Vinci's brothers Giovanni and Salvatore. Mele then confessed that he and Salvatore Vinci had killed the couple. Two years later, he was sentenced to 14 years and pronounced insane.

The Killer Strikes Again

On 14 September 1974, the bodies of Stefania Pettini and Pasquale Gentilcore were found. On 6 June 1981, the bodies of Carmela De Nuccio and her 30-year-old lover Giovanni Foggi, were discovered. The killer struck again on 23 October 1981, claiming Susanna Cambi and her boyfriend Stefano Baldi.

Florence, Italy – the scene of a 17–year murder spree by the 'Monster of Florence'.

Later Attacks

On 19 June 1982, the killer struck yet again, murdering Antonella Migliorini and her boyfriend Paolo Mainardi, who survived. Two West German boys perished on 9 September 1983, a young couple on 29 July 1984 and finally, on 8 September 1985, Jean-Michel Kraveichvili and Nadine Mauriot were murdered. What linked the cases was a .22 Beretta revolver and a surgical knife used to mutilate the bodies. Pietro Pacciani was convicted in 1994, but the verdict was overturned.

See The Californian Serial Killer p. 214

The Zodiac Killer (1969–74)

In the late 1960s and early 1970s, the Zodiac Killer, who chose his victims based on their astrological signs, killed at least five and claimed responsibility for 17 murders. The Zodiac Killer was a sexual sadist, who tortured his victims before murdering them.

Thousands of Suspects

On 4 July 1969, Darlene Ferrin was shot five times and her boyfriend Mike Mageau, although also shot four times, survived and saw the killer. In 1992, he positively identified Arthur Leigh Allen, a convicted child molester from Vallejo, California, who had been investigated by the police in the early 1980s and had always been a suspect. Allen died that year at the age of 58. DNA evidence, in any case, had cleared Allen, and over the course of the investigations since the last positively identified victim in 1969, some 2,500 people have been suspects.

The Zodiac Letters

Over the course of his murderous career, the Zodiac Killer sent at least 21 letters to the local press. All seemed to prove that he derived a considerable thrill from terrorizing the community. The Zodiac Killer would send his threats and communications in code, using a complex cipher, but this was broken by a high school history teacher. The last Zodiac letter arrived in 1974. Leads arrive on a daily basis and investigations are ongoing.

See Heriberto Seda p. 205

Bind Torture Kill (1974)

On 15 January 1974, Charles Otero returned to his home in Wichita, Kansas, to discover that his whole family had been butchered. Charles's father and mother had been tied up and strangled in their bedroom, as had his nine-year-old brother. His sister Josephine had been left naked, hanging from a pipe in the cellar. There was evidence that the killer had derived sexual gratification from the killings.

BTK Strangler

In 1975, a local newspaper received a strange note, directing them to a book deposited in a public library. Inside the book was a letter signed by the 'BTK Strangler'. It referred to the Otero killings. BTK was a direct quote from the book, which said 'bind them, torture them, kill them'. The police were already investigating a similar murder that had occurred on 4 April 1974. Kathryn Bright had been found in much the same state as Josephine Otero.

The End of the Murders

There was a lull until 17 March 1977, when the killer struck again. Shirley Vian was found in exactly the same manner. On 8 April 1977, Nancy Fox's life ended in similar circumstances. There was one more attempted murder, but this failed and the BTK never struck again.

See Jack the Stripper p. 210

The New Haven Murders (1975–90)

Between 1975 and 1990, a dozen young women, mainly prostitutes, were killed around New Haven, Connecticut. Seven of them may have been victims of the same killer, who strangled or stabbed them.

Roosevelt Bowden

The investigating team received a call from Florida linking the killings with some older, unsolved murders and naming Roosevelt Bowden. In 1978, Bowden had killed his daughter, but he was released from prison in 1986, and killing again in 1988. He was sentenced to death, but died from AIDS in April 1994. Five of the New Haven murders (1975–78) occurred before Bowden was in prison and two (1986) after he had been released. The three in August and September 1978 occurred whilst he was in prison.

The Californian Serial Killer (1979–86)

Between 1979 and 1986, 10 connected murders took place across four Californian coastal communities. Three Californian counties and four different law enforcement teams managed to link at least six of the crimes through DNA evidence found at the scenes. In the other four cases, whilst lacking DNA evidence, the same methods of killing suggest a link. Authorities believe the rapist killer may have been responsible for up to 50 rape attacks and 12 murders.

See The Monster of Florence p. 210

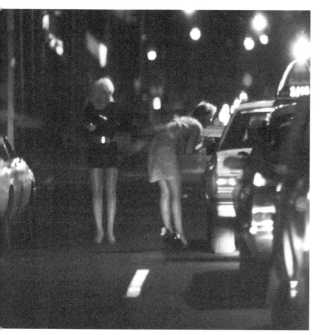

The Southside Slayer preyed on prostitutes, with as many as 20 victims in total.

The Southside Slayer (1984–87)

Between 1984 and 1987, at least 12 and possibly as many as 20 African-American drug-addicted prostitutes were murdered in the Los Angeles area. In 1993, despite the police denying the existence of a serial killer, they arrested an African-American policeman, who later proved to be unconnected with the crimes.

Suspect Speculation

The victims were subjected to torture with a knife before being strangled or stabbed to death. Some think that two convicted killers could be responsible for the murders, whilst others believe that it is the work of a lone man.

The Trail Goes Cold

The Southside Slayer has been inactive since 1987, so there have been no further leads, and it now appears that the scale of the investigation has been reduced; it is likely that the culprit will never be apprehended.

See Robert Pickton p. 226

The Juarez Serial Killer (1993–present)

Since 1993 around 260 young women, predominantly slim, with long hair and brown eyes, aged between 12 and 22, have disappeared from the Mexican border town of Ciudad Juarez. Local residents believe that the true number is closer to 400.

Trademarks of the Killer

Officially, the authorities put the figure at 76 – all have been raped, had their hands tied, their hair cut or had their breasts mutilated. Some have had their heads crushed or driven over by a car. Most of the women were killed on their return from work. Over time, the killings have become more brutal.

Still Out There

In November 2002, eight bodies were found and the police arrested two bus drivers, who confessed to raping and killing the eight women and three others. These were two men amongst the dozens arrested over the years, and every time the killings continued. The two new suspects later denied involvement and claimed that the police had tortured them into making the confessions. The state attorney general's office denies the torture allegations and continues to insist the men are guilty. As in the past, the new arrests did not seem to have stopped the killings. More bodies appeared after the bus drivers' arrest and continue to do so; in 2005 alone it is estimated 28 young women were murdered. The federal government has been criticized by Amnesty International for not doing enough to resolved the situation. There does not seem to be a motive for the murders, and they have been variously attributed to serial killers, drug cartels and domestic violence.

Murder Mysteries

Everyone loves a good murder mystery – as long as it is fictional. The cases in this section are real-life incidences of murders that baffled investigators and remain unsolved to this day.

The Bootlace Murders (1900)

In September 1900, Herbert Bennett arranged for his wife and child to visit Great Yarmouth, so that he could indulge in his affair with a young parlour-maid named Alice Meadows. On the night of 22 September, Bennett's wife was murdered on South Denes, Great Yarmouth; she had been strangled with a bootlace.

Execution of an Innocent Man?

Both Bennett and his wife had been involved in frauds and other moneymaking schemes, and she had booked into the lodgings under an assumed name. What damned Bennett at the trial was the fact that he had in his possession a gold chain that his wife had been wearing on the day she died. He was hanged in 1901, but in 1912, there was a near-identical murder on the same beach and doubts were raised as to his guilt.

See Christina Cochran p. 220

The Murder of Mabel Mayer (1927)

On 2 July 1927, 15-year-old Mabel Mayer from Oakland, California, was murdered close to her home. Her wristwatch had stopped at 10:06 and the body showed signs that she had been brutally beaten with a floorboard.

The Manhunt

The police hunted for a man witnesses described as being nearly 6 feet tall, between 35 and 40 years old and well built, with a dark complexion and long, matted hair. They linked the murder with a street robbery committed by a similar-looking man the previous Monday. Despite a police cordon and a degree of paranoia in Oakland for several weeks, the murderer of Mabel, known as 'Sunshine' to her friends and family, was never caught; neither was the man who had struck a few days earlier.

See The Valerie Percy Murder p. 218

The Brighton Trunk Murder (1933)

Tony Mancini lived at various addresses in Brighton with former dancer Violet Kaye. She earned her living from prostitution and Mancini was a waiter in a café. The couple had a

Brighton railway station as it would have looked at the time of the Brighton Trunk Murder.

public argument on 10 May 1933 when Violet accused Mancini of having affairs. Afterwards, Violet disappeared, Mancini claiming she had gone to work in Paris. Shortly afterwards, Mancini moved lodgings, taking with him a heavy trunk. On 17 June, a headless and legless body was found in a trunk at Brighton railway station; the victim was never identified, but amongst the suspects interviewed was Mancini. He panicked and fled to London, where he was arrested following the police discovery of Violet's decomposing body in the trunk at his Brighton lodgings.

Two Trunks, Two Bodies, Two Killers?

Although the two Brighton trunk murders may not have been related, Mancini had been undone by the investigations of the first murder. Mancini claimed he had found Violet's body on their bed when he had returned home and had panicked, claiming that as a convicted thief, the police would have automatically assumed his guilt. The jury returned a verdict of not guilty, but in a newspaper statement in 1976, Mancini admitted murdering Violet; the first trunk murder was never solved.

Valerie Percy Murder (1966)

On the night of 18 September 1966 in Kenilworth, Illinois, a murderer broke into the mansion home of Valerie Percy's father, who was campaigning for the US Senate. Valerie was brutally murdered for no apparent reason; she was found bludgeoned and stabbed to death. Police theorized that the murderer knew the Percy estate; the family dog had not barked and her father, Senator Charles Percy, was probably the intended victim.

See The Sir Harry Oakes Case p. 223

The Christine Demeter Case (1973)

In 1973 in Mississauga, Ontario, the former fashion model Christine Demeter was found bludgeoned to death in her home. Although her husband was later convicted of hiring an unknown killer to do away with his wife in order to collect a $1 million insurance policy, many of the facts of the case are unclear and the assailant was never arrested. The circumstances surrounding the blood-soaked garage in 1973 have never been fully explained.

See The Trial of Alfred John Monson p. 222

Fashion model Christine Demeter, who was found bludgeoned to death in her home in 1973.

The Tammy Zywicki Case (1992)

Tammy Zywicki was last seen alive on 23 August 1992, when she left Illinois, heading for university. Her body was found on 1 September in the Missouri countryside; she had been sexually assaulted and repeatedly stabbed. Witnesses suggested the killer was white, between 35 and 40 and over 6 feet tall, with dark, bushy hair. One suspect, Lonnie Bierbodt, was cleared. There is still a $150,000 reward for information leading to an arrest.

Brown's Chicken and Seafood Killings (1993)

Seven employees at Brown's chicken and seafood restaurant in Palatine, Illinois, were murdered on the night of 8 January 1993. The police made the grisly discovery several hours after closing time; the bodies were found in two walk-in refrigerators in the kitchen area. The only tangible evidence was some bullet fragments and the fact that the safe had been robbed; the electricity had also been turned off. Police never found the perpetrators.

Under Suspicion

In many murder cases, there are obvious prime suspects – people with means and motive – but finding the evidence against them is not always easy. Sometimes, it is not enough to secure a conviction, and a potential killer is allowed to go free, leaving the case officially unsolved.

Christina Cochran (1843)

Christina Cochran married John Gilmour in Ayrshire in 1843. Within six weeks, he was dead. He was buried, but Christina's flight to America caused suspicion; she was intercepted and her husband's body was exhumed. Tests revealed that he had died from arsenic poisoning. Witnesses suggested Christina had bought the poison herself or had sent a maid to buy it for her. The evidence in court was contradictory and inconclusive. Christina was found not guilty and it was suggested that John may have accidentally poisoned himself. They returned a verdict of not proven; Cochran spent the next 62 years of her life an unattached widow.

Bravo, Florence (1876)

After separating from her first husband, Florence maintained a long-term relationship with her close friend Dr Gully, but in 1875, she married Charles Bravo. On 18 April 1876, Charles was struck down by what was believed to be arsenic poisoning, and his death resulted in two inquests and much gossip. It transpired that arsenic was

Charles Bravo, poisoned by an unknown hand in 1876.

not the poison in question but that it was antimony, a drug used in Florence's stables. The inquests were sure that Charles had been murdered but there was insufficient evidence to bring charges against anyone. Theories abounded; Gully's reputation was ruined and Florence died an alcoholic in September 1878.

Bartlett, Adelaide (1886)

French-born Adelaide married Edwin Bartlett in 1875. Edwin was rather a strange character, something of a hypochondriac – he had all his teeth sawn off at the roots and was perhaps suffering from syphilis – and he showed little interest in sleeping with his wife, although they did have a child that was stillborn.

Adelaide – Accused and Acquitted

In 1885, Edwin engaged George Dyson, a man of education, to tutor his wife. Dyson and Adelaide began an affair. On 27 December, Dyson bought chloroform so that Adelaide could use it on Edwin should he make sexual advances towards her. However, her husband had fallen ill a few days before and was already bedridden. On 1 January 1886, he died; the postmortem the following day revealed chloroform in his stomach. Adelaide was arrested and charged with his murder, but no one could explain how the chloroform had got into his stomach. She was acquitted and disappeared from public view; she may have returned to France or emigrated to America.

Adelaide Bartlett, who was acquitted after an inconclusive trial.

The Trial of Alfred John Monson (1893)

First, we have Major Hambrough, compelled to come and admit... proven" is always returned as a compromise. The defence has opened very quietly, with evidence on... Hambrough worth anoth...

MONSON A J DEC 1893
ALFRED JOHN
TRIAL FOR KILLING MR CECIL
THE ARDLAMONT CASE.
FOTOMAS INDEX
020 8776 2772

for the prisoner are
Dr. Hay, Professor

The trial of Alfred John Monson, accused of murdering Cecil Hambrough.

The trial of Alfred Monson, accused of murdering Cecil Hambrough, was a tale of fraud, money-lending and deceit. The killing occurred on the Ardlamont Estate in Argyllshire on 10 August 1893. Monson, having taken out insurance on Cecil's life, faked Cecil's suicide to cash in the insurance. Cecil's father, a near-bankrupt landowner, had become embroiled with Monson and a money-lender called Tottenham, and the financial dealings became more complex since Cecil had assigned payments, in the event of his death, to Monson's wife. The jury heard that on the day before Cecil's death, Monson had tried to drown him; the prosecution was largely due to insistence from the insurance company. Circumstantially, there were motives, but certain peculiarities of the Scottish court produced a verdict of not proven.

The Julia Wallace Case (1931)

William Herbert Wallace returned home on the night of 19 January 1931 to find his wife Julia dead. Her head had been smashed with a poker, and a mackintosh, heavily stained with blood, had been partly burned.

Convicted and Reprieved

William, a Prudential Assurance agent in Liverpool, had gone out to meet a Mr Qualtrough, but the address did not exist and Qualtrough never appeared. The police charged William with Julia's murder and, in a heavily biased trial in April 1931, he was found guilty and sentenced to death. The sentence was quashed by the Lord Chief Justice the following month, making legal history.

Wallace returned to work, but to his dying day, he was plagued with gossip, innuendo and ill-health, dying prematurely on 26 February 1933. Further enquiries have uncovered no additional evidence.

See The Bootlace Murders p. 216

Barney, Elvira (1932)

On 31 May 1932, Elvira Barney, a wealthy socialite living in Knightsbridge, reported the shooting of her lover, Michael Stephen. The couple had been seen arguing and Barney explained that she had intended to commit suicide, but the gun had accidentally gone off, killing Stephen. She was found not guilty in court but just four years later, she committed suicide in a Paris hotel.

The Sir Harry Oakes Case (1943)

The body of American-born Canadian citizen Sir Harry Oakes, a multi-millionaire, was found in his home in Nassau in the Bahamas on 8 July 1943. His body had

Alfred de Marigny is escorted by police, accused of the murder of Sir Harry Oakes.

been battered and burnt. The Duke of Windsor was then the governor of the islands and called in two detectives from the Miami Police Department to investigate. As a result, Oakes' son-in-law, Alfred de Marigny, was charged and tried for the murder.

The case was horribly mishandled and he was acquitted. Indeed, the precise nature of the weapon that had caused the fatal wounds was never established, nor were the feathers scattered around the body explained. Several attempts were made to reopen the case, but to no avail, and no further light has ever been shed on the crime.

See The Karin Cookie Kupcinet Case p. 229

The Charles Walton Case (1945)

On 14 February 1945, 74-year-old Charles Walton headed off towards Meon Hill on Potter's Farm in Lower Quinton, Warwickshire, to do some hedge-cutting; he never returned home. His family called the police and that night they found his body. His throat had been slashed with his own scythe, which had been left sticking out of his neck. Cut into the skin of his neck and chest was a cross.

Ritual Murder

The case was not easy to solve and celebrated detective Robert Fabian was called in to investigate. He discovered that the death had the hallmarks of a ritual killing related to witchcraft. The one lead he had was that an Italian prisoner of war working in a nearby camp was seen washing his hands in a ditch. He also had bloodstains on his coat, but he refused to answer any questions. This later turned out to be rabbit's blood.

Fabian claimed he knew who had committed the murder; it was Albert Potter, to whom Walton had lent a considerable amount of money. Potter simply could not pay it back and killed the old man, faking the witchcraft connection. However, he was never brought to trial.

See The Trial of Alfred John Monson p. 222

The Moonlight Murders (1946)

On the night of 22 February 1946, Mary Jeanne Larey and Jimmy Hollis narrowly survived an attack by a 'phantom-like' murderer in Texarkana, on the Texas-Arkansas border. One month later, Richard Griffin and Polly Ann Moore were found murdered; she had also been raped. On 13 April, Betty Jo Booker and Jerry Atkins were murdered in a similar fashion.

The Phantom Killer

Three hundred suspects were brought in for questioning, but on 3 May, the phantom struck again, killing Virgil Starks and seriously wounding his wife Katy in their home. The police finally focused on a man called Youell Swinney. After his arrest, the killings ceased for good. Swinney was tried and sentenced to life in 1947, but in 1974, his conviction was overturned and, due to a legal loophole, he was released. Technically, the case still remains unsolved.

See The Axe-Man of New Orleans p. 209

The Murder of Stanley Setty (1949)

Brian Donald Hume, discharged from the RAF, set up an electrical business in Golders Green, London. In 1949, he met car-dealer Stanley Setty, who was last seen alive in October whilst

Sydney Tiffin indicates the place where he found the dismembered torso of Stanley Setty.

carrying £1,000 in cash in his pocket. Shortly afterwards, his headless body was found rolled in a carpet in the marshes near Southend-on-Sea; his body appeared to have been thrown out of an aircraft. Hume had hired a plane from Elstree airfield and was arrested; in January 1950, he faced two trials; the first was abandoned when the judge became ill and the second when the jury failed to reach a verdict. Ultimately, Hume admitted being an accessory after the fact to murder and was jailed for 12 years; he blamed the killing on three other men.

Pickton, Robert (1983–2002)

In July 2003, Robert Pickton, a former pig farmer from British Columbia, was formally charged with 15 counts of murder. He had been finally linked to a series of 63 disappearances of drug addicts and prostitutes in the Vancouver area, over a period of nearly 20 years.

Former pig farmer Robert Pickton, charged with the murder of 15 women.

Serial Killer

The police mounted a raid on his home on 6 February 2002 and retrieved sufficient evidence to charge Pickton with two murders. In October 2002, he was charged with an additional 13 murders. Investigations continued and in 2007, he was sentenced to life imprisonment for these and a series of prostitute murders that had formerly been unsolved. At his trial in 2007, he confessed to killing 49 people.

Gathering Evidence

At the height of the investigations, over 50 anthropologists were deployed at his farm, sifting through soil and trying to uncover the remains of bodies. It is believed that after murdering the women, Pickton disposed of their bodies in a wood-pulping machine, then mixed their body parts with pig feed. Police found women's clothing that may link Pickton directly to the disappearances. Many of the victims appear to have been Native American women.

See The Juarez Serial Killer p. 215

The Murder of Jaidyn Leskie (1998)

Toddler Jaidyn Leskie's body was found in a dam near Moe in Australia on 1 January 1998, after he disappeared in mysterious circumstances. His mother's former boyfriend, Greg Domaszewicz, who was babysitting Jaidyn when he disappeared, was charged with the murder, but was acquitted by a Supreme Court jury in December 1998.

Ongoing Investigations

The deputy state coroner closed the case in 2001, after holding a closed-door inquiry and producing a two-page report outlining the previously known facts about the death. Nonetheless, police detectives attached to his office continued to investigate the circumstances of the toddler's death, taking new statements from witnesses involved, as well as new DNA and other forensic tests. In July 2003, it was announced that there will be a new public enquiry.

See The Murder of Georgina Moore p. 186

Famous Faces

Some of the best-known mysteries are those relating to celebrities. Unexplained deaths or disappearances garner massive media coverage and capture the imagination of the public. Despite all the investigations and conspiracy theories, these cases will probably never be solved.

Marilyn Monroe, whose suspicious death has never been resolved.

The Death of Marilyn Monroe (1962)

On 4 August 1962, the body of the world's most glamorous film star was found on her bed in her Los Angeles home. She had died from a massive dose of Nembutal and chloral-hydrate. Officially, the inquest delivered a verdict of probable suicide.

Conspiracy Theories

The truth may have been far more sinister and, indeed, the favourite conspiracy theory is that Marilyn was murdered by lethal injection because she knew too much following her affairs with both President John F. Kennedy and his brother, the US attorney general Robert Kennedy.

Accidental Death?

Marilyn had been born Norma Jean Baker in 1926 and had been through some difficult times. She had married Joe DiMaggio in 1954 and Arthur Miller, the playwright, in 1956, in addition to her much-publicized affairs with the Kennedys. There had been accidental overdoses in the past, as the simple Los Angeles girl struggled to cope with her fame. Robert Kennedy admitted he had been at Marilyn's home on the afternoon of her death and that a doctor who had accompanied him had injected the actress with a tranquillizer. Details about the rest of the day, and exactly how she died, remain unclear.

The Karyn 'Cookie' Kupcinet Case (1963)

On the evening of 30 November 1963, the naked body of an actress known as Cookie was found in her West Hollywood apartment. She had last been seen alive three days before. What is particularly bizarre is that she made a distraught phone call to a telephone operator, claiming that President Kennedy was about to be assassinated, 20 minutes before he was. Conspiracy theorists believe that she was the victim of a clean-up squad that went around killing potential witnesses. She had called from a phone box rather than her home, possibly believing that her call could be traced. Whether her death was linked to the assassination is still not known. Her father knew Jack Ruby in the 1940s, but had no connection with him in 1963.

See Jack Ruby p. 20

Lord Lucan (1974)

Lord Lucan, a professional gambler, disappeared on 8 November 1974, and has never been seen again. It is believed that Lucan had intended to murder his estranged wife at their home in Belgravia on the night of 7 November.

The Facts of the Case

At 9.20 p.m., Lady Lucan went downstairs to see why the children's nanny, Sandra Rivett, was taking so long to make tea. She was hit over the head and began struggling with a man who she later claimed was her husband. Shortly afterwards, Sandra's body was found in a US mail sack, with a piece of lead piping lying beside it, in the basement. Lady Lucan raised the alarm and in the time it took her to come back with neighbours, Lucan had disappeared. Lucan drove to friends in Sussex, claiming he had attacked the man who had struck his wife and that she had believed him to be the attacker. Shortly after 1 a.m., he drove from his friends' home, saying he would remain out of the picture until the situation calmed down. His abandoned car was found near Newhaven; in the boot was another US mail sack and a similar length of lead piping.

See The Bootlace Murders p. 216

Sandra Rivett, nanny to the three Lucan children at the time of her murder.

The Jill Dando Case (1999)

On 26 April 1999, Jill Dando, a 37-year-old TV presenter, was shot dead on the doorstep of her home in Fulham, London. Forensic science discovered a particle of gunpowder only 11 microns in size. The tiny particle was found on a coat belonging to the suspect.

Forensics Success

In the trial, an expert explained that when a gun is fired, minute traces of the discharge residue are found on the body or clothes of the shooter. The particle could have been produced by the type of cartridge used in the murder; the particle was discovered over a year after the coat came into police hands. One of the objections was the possibility of cross-contamination; in other words, could the particle have found its way on to the coat by being in proximity to other evidence? The experts described the extreme operating conditions to eliminate this situation.

The Conviction Overturned

The minute particle helped to convict Barry George; in December 2002, his appeal request was turned down, but in 2006, his lawyers appealed claiming new evidence. A retrial began in 2008, at the end of which George was acquitted. If indeed he was not the killer, Dando's murderer is now unlikely ever to be caught.

See Firearms Testing p. 242

CCTV footage shows TV presenter Jill Dando in a shop, 40 minutes before her death.

10

investigative techniques

& punishment

Crime-Scene Science

Under normal circumstances, the first police to arrive at a crime scene are the uniformed officers. Whatever the crime, there will be evidence to collect from the scene, which may require the services of specialists.

Crime-Scene Investigation

Once the crime scene has been secured, a minute search begins to see whether the perpetrator has left any traces. There are various crime-scene kits that are used to collect latent fingerprints or trace evidence. Fingerprinting kits may be required, as may casting kits, in the case of footprints or vehicle tyre prints.

A police van undergoes investigation following an attempted hijack.

CSI Tools

At the scene of crime, laser pointers are often used to track the trajectory of a bullet that may be lodged in furniture or the victim. With the use of angle-finders, the precise location where the shot was fired can be discovered. The evidence collected at the scene of the crime is correctly labelled and then dispatched to a laboratory for processing. One of the major hazards in investigating a crime scene is the danger of the police themselves contaminating the scene inadvertently; protective clothing, therefore, is always worn.

See Luminol p. 237

Fingerprints and Other Impressions

The multiple murderer Richard Ramirez was finally betrayed by his fingerprints. This area of investigation began to develop in Britain in the late 1890s. One of the first times it was used was in the case of a murder in Deptford in 1905. The Stratton brothers left just one thumbprint at the scene, condemning them to be hanged.

Fingerprint Specialists

Each fingerprint is unique, with its own mixture of arches or ridges, oval formations and loops. A perpetrator could leave visible prints, perhaps in ink or blood, latent prints, which can later be recovered, or prints left on soft surfaces. Experienced fingerprint specialists can retrieve fingerprints and then compare them to automated fingerprint identification systems housed on computers. The process may take days.

Other Prints

Other prints may be left at a scene, as in the case of the murder of Juana Gillette who, according to her husband, had died suddenly. Investigators found a plastic bag and by turning it inside out, there was a discernable impression of the dead woman's face. In this case, her husband, who had suffocated her, was undone by a nose print. Ear prints are now also used, as are footprint impressions.

Print-Lifting

The first 'superglue' was introduced in the 1970s as a fast-bonding adhesive. Since then, it has been used by doctors instead of stitches to close wounds. A further, unintended use of the glue has been discovered to lift 'impossible' prints on plastic bags, car windows and on bodies. The glue contains a chemical called cyanoacrylate, which is attracted to amino acids, fats or proteins that can be left on surfaces by human touch. The glue is heated in a metal container and the vapour produced attaches itself to the human residue and forms a hard coating.

Uses of Print-Lifting

The coated prints can then be removed, dyed to make them visible and then compared to known prints on a database. The technique can be used for small objects such as bullet casings, as well as bodies, telephones and other surfaces that are not ideal for conventional print identification.

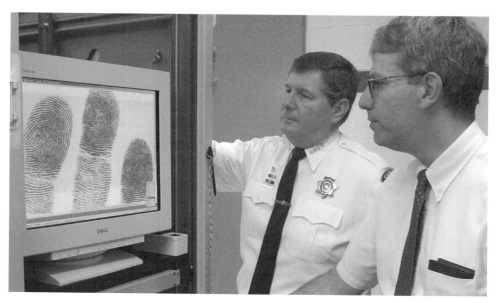

Detectives study fingerprints displayed on a Live Scan fingerprint system.

Hair and Dust Analysis

Human hair at a murder or crime scene can tell much about the victim or the perpetrator. Its presence suggests contact between the victim and a suspect. Analysis of the hair itself allows the scientist to identify racial differences, the presence of poison or dyes, and of course the roots may yield DNA.

The Uniqueness of Dust

Dust found at a crime scene can be almost as unique as DNA. Microscopic fragments of clothing fibres, pollen, house dust or building dust can suggest where a crime may have been committed, or can help indicate the normal surroundings of a suspect. The assortment of trace materials, such as hair, fibre, insect scales and pollen, make each building's dust unique. Dust related to work or a particular industry may also prove useful.

See Trace-Evidence Analysis p. 240

Luminol

Luminol is a chemical that reacts with haemoglobin and can detect blood at one part per million. It glows greenish-blue when it comes into contact with blood. Scene-of-crime investigators spray the chemical over a wide area, in as close to near-darkness as possible. When a photograph is taken of the area, the camera's flash will pick up the glow.

Uses of Luminol

Luminol does react to some metals, cleaning products and paints, but the reaction is different and the glow fades more quickly compared to blood. Once the blood has been identified, it can then be tested to see whether it is human. The glowing areas can also show investigators whether a body has been dragged across a surface, or the direction in which the victim was shot, through blood spatters.

See Serology p. 239

Investigative Science

Much forensic science takes place in the laboratory after evidence has been gathered. The tiniest traces of organic or even inorganic material can reveal much information about the killer, the murder weapon, the time and place of death and many other factors, which can be used to convict a suspect.

DNA Testing

In 1985, British researcher Alec Jeffreys discovered that, with the exception of identical twins, each human being has unique DNA. DNA profiling allows the scientist to separate an individual's unique fragments from those that are common in all. DNA is found in white blood cells, which can be taken from hair follicles, skin, blood, saliva and semen.

These cells, found on the clothing of a burglar, could help to convict him.

Improvements in Technology

As DNA technology has improved, researchers have been able to narrow down matches from several thousand people to an individual. DNA can be left at the murder scene accidentally by the perpetrator in the form of hair or flakes of skin. As long as the sample is immediately tested or deep frozen, even the smallest trace of skin cells can be used.

See Peter Dupas p. 105

Serology

Serology is the study of serums, derived from blood, sweat, saliva, semen or faeces. The minute traces of serum can be analysed, and scientists know how bodies and blood behave in certain circumstances. In the case of a wound that may or may not lead to a death, the blood will spray in particular directions and specific distances according to the atmospheric pressure, humidity or temperature. Within the blood itself, there are a number of standardized groups based on the red blood cells. Types A and O are the most common and AB is the rarest. An identification of the type of blood, particularly if it is not the blood of a victim, can be most telling and may narrow down the search for the perpetrator.

A murder weapon is tested for the victim's blood group.

Advances in Serology

Blood typing now also includes the different types of enzymes and proteins. Again, in order to ensure that there is no cross-contamination between the investigators and the blood traces, extreme measures are taken to ensure that the evidence is not corrupted. In the event that attempts have been made to clean away blood traces at a scene, the use of Luminol can pinpoint where the blood traces can be found and then samples can be taken for further analysis.

See Luminol p. 237

Trace-Evidence Analysis

Since the human body is constantly shedding hair, skin or fragments of fingernail, a suspect may inadvertently leave some of this trace evidence behind at the crime scene.

DNA Evidence

Clearly, blood will provide the opportunity for DNA analysis and for blood-typing. Saliva, which can also be found on cigarettes, envelopes or glasses and cups, will yield DNA. Sperm again provides DNA and, since it remains alive for a short period of time, can also help indicate when the attack was carried out. Fingernails on each person have unique patterns and, since the mid-1970s, individual matches have been made and used as evidence in court. Hair roots offer DNA and they can also show whether a struggle took place at the crime scene. Skin cells, perhaps left underneath the fingernails of a victim, can again be linked through DNA to the perpetrator.

Particle Evidence

Collectively, hair strands, dirt particles, glass fragments, fibres from clothing and paint smears are known as 'mute witnesses'. They are microscopic remnants of a person or an object that was present at the crime scene. Unless the perpetrator takes the ultimate step of wearing a full body suit, it is almost certain that something of them will be left behind.

See DNA Testing p. 238

Fibre Analysis

Minute fibre analysis can link a suspect to a particular crime scene, either where they have left traceable fibres, or when they have carried fibres away from the scene. In 1982, Kristen Harrison was found raped and strangled in Ohio; there were orange fibres in her hair. Scientists surmised they were carpet fibres. Sometime later, another woman was abducted and held prisoner; she was tortured but escaped and she had the same orange fibres in her hair. They were traced to a manufacturer and only 74 yards had been sold in the Ohio area, allowing the police to arrest rapist and murderer Robert Buel.

See The Sarah Payne Case p. 100

Autopsies

In New York alone, it has been estimated that there are around 8,000 autopsies, or post-mortems, each year. In the case of a suspicious death, a minute dissection and examination of the body is essential in the hunt for evidence.

Reasons for Autopsies

In effect, the first function of an autopsy is to establish the cause of death. Once this has been done, trace elements are collected from the body and then the surgeon begins to dissect the corpse itself, exposing all the internal organs. X-rays of injuries are taken in order to identify trajectory paths of bullets or knife wounds. Blood samples are taken. The organs, including the brain, are examined and weighed. By the end of the process, the surgeon should be able to provide investigators with a precise cause and time of death, an indication of whether the body has been moved and, once various tests have been returned, the probable age, whether poisons or drugs were in the system and information that could lead to the identification of an unknown corpse.

Autopsy Results

The autopsy results should provide evidence for a future prosecution, perhaps linking a suspect to the corpse by various means, such as gunshot residue, trace elements or evidence of sexual assault.

See Serology p. 239

Toxicology

Toxicology may be an integral part of an autopsy, as it is the series of chemical tests that aim to detect the substances that an individual has ingested prior to death. A toxicology test may be able to identify the precise type of poison used to kill a victim, identifying the differences in the condition of the body as a result of the poisoning and perhaps the discovery of minute traces of the poison itself. Every poison has a different series of chemical reactions with the body and affects particular organs in different ways. More common forms of toxicology tests include the presence of alcohol, prescription drugs, soft and hard illegal drugs and the presence of lead in the body or its organs.

Forensic Entomology

A dead body will inevitably attract flies and maggots. Forensic entomology examines the presence of insects and in doing so, the scientist can determine the victim's time of death or how long the body has been in a particular place. Integral to the investigation is assessment of how far into their life cycle particular insects have developed. Blowflies, for example, lay eggs within 48 hours of death, these eggs then become larvae between 16 and 25 hours. The larvae become pupae within six to 12 days; this all, of course, depends on the ambient temperature. 'Foreign' insects to a particular area indicate that the body has been moved. The presence of beetles that eat bones will again indicate how long the body has been in situ.

See Autopsies p. 241

Firearms Testing

The science of firearms testing or interpretation allows the scientist to compare bullets and match them to a specific firearm. It can also estimate how far the bullet travelled before it hit its target. Above all, it can detect gunpowder residue around the wounds of a victim and on the person who used the gun. By using an electron microscope, tiny particles of the gunshot residue can be traced to clothing and to skin, even if the clothing has been washed or a considerable time has elapsed since the event.

German forensic entymologist Mark Benecke at work.

Matching the Bullet to the Gun

Each bullet fired from a specific gun has unique grooves and marks made on it while it travels down the rifled barrel. By firing a test shot with the weapon, analysts are able to positively state whether a particular bullet was fired by a particular gun.

See The Jill Dando Case p. 230

Forensic Handwriting

Specialists who examine handwriting fall into two main categories. Forensic document examiners compare handwriting samples and make an assessment as to whether they were written by the same person. Graphologists look at particular aspects of the handwriting and relate these to particular personality traits, enabling the investigators to build up a profile of the suspect. Handwriting analysis can also identify the speed of the writing by examining the beginning and end of each word.

See David Berkowitz p. 62

Procedures on Suspects

For decades now, psychological profiling has been used by law enforcement agencies as a way of working out the kind of person they are looking for or if a captured suspect fits this profile. Other methods are used too, once in custody, to determine a suspect's guilt or innocence.

Psychological Profiling

In the 1950s, psychologists began theorizing that certain criminals had similar behavioural patterns and personalities. The FBI began using this kind of profiling extensively in the 1970s, and profilers began to look for unique details that could indicate the perpetrator's background, experience or motivations. The profile can also suggest the age, lifestyle, habits and employment of the perpetrator, along with gender, race, physical size and marital status.

Criminal Behaviour

Profiling can be very specific and there is now a national computer database in the US that can be used to cross-reference and connect similar crimes across the country. The profiler can determine whether certain behaviours link crimes together. In the US, there are around 30 professional criminal profilers, who concentrate on the study of the characteristics of some of the most violent and persistent criminals in the country. Although psychological profiling has its detractors who suggest that more traditional forms of investigative techniques reap greater benefits, profiling helps to narrow the hunt. In recent years, profilers have been used in many of the biggest cases, helping investigators to recognize patterns in the behaviour of a perpetrator and match these to potential suspects. In most major crimes, both in the US and the UK, profilers are integral to the team.

See Kenneth Bianchi and Angelo Buono p. 58

Lie Detectors and Polygraphs

A suspect subjected to these tests has a strap around the abdomen and chest to record the breathing rate, another strap around the bicep to measure blood pressure and electrodes on the fingertips to measure perspiration. The subject is then asked baseline questions, to which the answers are already known, such as their age or sex. These measurements are then used to compare with the suspect's reactions to other, more penetrating questions regarding a particular crime.

Cheating the Polygraph

The technique is not 100 per cent reliable, although the new computerized polygraphs are considerably more accurate. Accomplished liars, or those who can control their stress levels, are able to trick the test. Under normal circumstances, the tests are only admissible if the judge agrees. New developments include using a voice analyser and a brainwave monitor to back up the test.

See Roland McDonald p. 152

Brain Fingerprinting

Brain-fingerprint testing has proved to be accurate in over 170 tests, which actually included criminal cases. It determines whether information is present or absent in the brain and is able to identify, by measuring brainwaves, the recognition or non-recognition of aspects of a crime. A suspect can be tested for knowledge that only the perpetrator would know. It can place someone at the crime scene, or prove that they were not there.

Uses of Brain Fingerprinting

In pre-court tests, the subject can be asked questions about the crime without the danger of them having knowledge of it through court proceedings. The tests can also be used for convicted criminals, as even information that they have picked up from the trial or press coverage can be distinguished from their own knowledge.

Execution Methods

Today, the death sentence is passed only in extreme cases, but it was not always that way. Historically, criminals – or even just those disliked by society – were summarily tried and executed in all manner of ways. Methods of execution have become more 'humane' over the years, and in some cases, death-row inmates may even choose how they wish to die.

Burning

Burning at the stake was undoubtedly the most popular means of dealing with religious heretics and those believed to be witches in England during the sixteenth century. It was considered an appropriate method of execution, as the flames were thought to cleanse the soul.

Death by Fire

Theoretically, the smoke should render the victim unconscious or asphyxiated before the flames began to burn their bodies. In practice, however, this was not always the case and the victim would, quite literally, be burned to death. In some cases, a rope was attached to the condemned's neck and, as a favour, this would be stretched to either strangle or render the victim unconscious before the fire consumed their bodies.

Catherine Hayes is burned at the stake for the murder of her husband in 1725.

At Smithfield in London, a further mercy or privilege was often accorded to the condemned in the shape of a small bag of gunpowder attached to the neck. As the flames licked up around the torso, the head would literally be blown off.

Hanging

For centuries, the sight of a criminal dangling at the end of a rope, dying from slow strangulation, was popular entertainment in many countries around the world. It was a cheap means of execution: a tree with a convenient bough, a wooden beam protruding from a dwelling or a purpose-built scaffold all afforded the means by which the criminal could be dispatched.

British Hangings

The last two men to be hanged in Britain were murderers Peter Allen and Gwynne Evans, on 13 August 1964; the last woman was Ruth Ellis on 13 July 1955; by this time, such executions were carried out within prison walls and were no longer public entertainment.

US Hangings

In the US, there have been only three hangings since 1977, as this method of execution has largely been replaced by electrocution. Three states retain the hanging option: Delaware, New Hampshire and Washington. As in the latter years in Britain, the 'drop' is based on the condemned person's weight, enough to deliver sufficient force to break the neck. Death is achieved by the dislocation of the third and fourth cervical vertebrae.

See Ruth Ellis p. 137

Drawing and Quartering

While the rope or the axe was reserved for lesser mortals, the ultimate execution method was only meted out on those who had committed high treason. Those who had plotted against the king or the country could expect no mercy in a punishment that amounted to public butchery – drawing and quartering.

How It Worked

In effect, this meant the criminal would be partially hung, taken down, then disembowelled (with the intestines being burned before the miscreant) and then decapitated by a blow with an axe. After this, the body would be quartered – parts of the body were sent to the four corners of the kingdom as a stark warning of the fate for others who considered high treason.

The unfortunate regicides, executed in 1660, were hung, drawn and quartered.

Beheading

In the UK, the last time a criminal was beheaded was in 1820; for some time, it had been reserved for those who had committed high treason. The last unfortunate victims were the men behind the infamous Cato Street Conspiracy, who had plotted to slaughter the whole of the British Cabinet.

The Axeman

The axe needed to be accurate and an accomplished 'headsman' could decapitate with a single blow. Typically, the condemned would be required to place their head on a solid block of oak designed to facilitate the executioner's task. It was in this way that Lady Jane Grey, Anne Boleyn, Catherine Howard and Charles I were dispatched.

See Hanging p. 247

Electrocution

In 1888, New York became the first US state to adopt electrocution, first used in the execution of William Kemmler in 1890. By 1949, this majority of US states had adopted the method and between 1930 and 1980, it was the most popular method. Presently, only Nebraska uses electrocution as its sole method of execution.

The beheading of a leader of the 1358 French insurrection, under the king's orders.

The Electric Chair

The condemned person is strapped to an oak chair placed on a rubber net. A leg-piece is fixed to the right calf, to which an electrode is attached. A metal headpiece is then put on, with a leather hood to cover the face. Another electrode is fixed to this contraption. At the appointed time, the safety switch is closed and a current of 2,300 volts is passed through the body for eight seconds; this is followed by a 22-second burst of 1,000 volts and finally, another 2,300 volts for another eight seconds. If the condemned is not dead, the process is repeated.

Problems with Electrocution

The most common problem with electrocution as a means of execution is that it can fail to cause death instantly and therefore it becomes necessary to repeat the process several times. In addition, the body suffers burning at the point of contact with the electrodes. As a result of these issues, electrocution has largely been replaced with lethal injection.

Gas

An airtight chamber is used, in which a chair with restraints is placed. The condemned person is strapped into the chair (chest, arms, waist and ankles) and a hood is placed over the head. Three keys are required to trigger the mechanism, which causes cyanide pellets to be released from a container under the chair; these fall into a second container with a sulphuric acid solution. A lethal gas is created by the chemical reaction. Death usually takes place within 6–18 minutes of the release of the gas. A heart monitor attached to the condemned indicates the time of death.

An Agonizing Death

Ammonia is then pumped into the chamber to neutralize the gas and then exhaust fans remove the fumes from the chamber, a process which takes around 30 minutes. Normally, the condemned loses consciousness within seconds, but if the victim holds their breath, then they suffer an agonizing death during which they suffer convulsions. As a result of this, this method has been rarely used by US standards – only 11 times since 1976.

Firing Squad

The firing squad was a fate usually reserved for military deserters or spies, with the firing squad itself made up of trained marksmen. In the US, three states officially authorize the use of the firing squad: Idaho, Oklahoma and Utah. The most recent examples of death by this method include Gary Gilmore (1977), John Albert Taylor (1996) and Ronnie Lee Gardner (2010).

The Shooters

A five-person firing squad (police officers) are selected and armed with rifles, and positioned some 6 m (20 ft) away from the condemned person, who has been strapped into a specially designed chair. A Velcro circle is placed over their heart. The firing squad takes up position behind a wall and fires a volley on order through ports (holes) in the wall. One of the squad has been given a blank cartridge, so that each man can take comfort that he may not have fired the fatal shot. If the condemned is not dispatched by the volley, then the officer in charge delivers a pistol shot to the head.

See Gary Gilmore p. 116

Lethal Injection

Lethal injection was first considered in the US in 1888, but it was not until 1977 that the first state, Oklahoma, adopted the method. The first use of the lethal injection took place in Texas in 1982, with the execution of Charlie Brooks.

The Drug Combination

Lethal injection actually involves three different drugs. The first is sodium thiopental (or sodium pentothal), which renders the condemned person unconscious. The second is then delivered, pancuronium bromide, a muscle relaxant that effectively paralyses the diaphragm and lungs. Finally, potassium chloride is used, which induces cardiac arrest. Before the intravenous lines are inserted, a sedative may well be given to the condemned. Two intravenous lines are usually put in; the second as a back up should there be a blockage in the first line.

Use of the Lethal Injection

Currently, 18 US states and the federal government can authorize the use of lethal injection as the sole means of execution. Some 19 other states use lethal injection as an execution alternative. Since 1976, 81 per cent of US executions have been carried out by lethal injection. Recently, questions have been raised about its efficiency.

See John Wayne Gacy Jr p. 59

Resources

Further Reading

Black, Ray, et al, *Killers in Cold Blood*, Futura, 2007

Castelden, Rodney, *Great Unsolved Crimes*, Futura, 2007

Davies, Carol Anne, *Women Who Kill: Profiles of Female Serial Killers*, Allison & Busby, 2002

Donnelly, Paul, *501 Most Notorious Crimes*, Bounty Books, 2009

Douglas, John E. and Mark Olshaker, *The Cases That Haunt Us*, Simon & Schuster, 2003

Harding, David, et al, *Rampage: The Social Roots of School Shootings*, Basic Books, 2005

Jakubowski, Maxim, *The Mammoth Book of Jack the Ripper*, Robinson, 2008

Katz, Helena, *Cold Cases: Famous Unsolved Mysteries, Crimes and Disappearances in America*, Greenwood Press, 2010

Murray, William, *Serial Killers*, Canary Press, 2007

Paul, Jonathan, *When Kids Kill: Unthinkable Crimes of Lost Innocence*, True Crime, 2006

Wilkes, Roger, *The Giant Book of Unsolved Crimes*, Magpie, 2006

Williams, Anne, *Criminal Masterminds*, Futura, 2007

Wilson, Colin, *The Mammoth Book of True Crime*, Robinson Publishing, 1998

Websites

www.casebook.org
A website dedicated to information about the most notorious killer of all time – Jack the Ripper.

www.chicagohs.org/history/capone.html
Find out all about the most famous gangster of all time – Al Capone; with a biography, photographs, and how the police brought him down.

www.exploreforensics.co.uk
A UK-based website all about forensic science. Here, you can find out about the different fields of forensics and review some specific cases where scientific evidence helped catch a killer.

www.fbi.gov/wanted.htm
This is the website of the FBI's Most Wanted list. You can read all about the criminals still sought by the FBI, with photographs, descriptions and information about their crimes.

www.met.police.uk/history
The history section of the Metropolitan Police's website, with a section on famous cases, such as the Brighton murders, Jack the Ripper and the Kray twins, and information about the Met itself.

www.murderuk.com
All aspects of murder are covered in this website that collates information about homicide in the UK, with sections on historical and current cases.

Index